REGENTS RENAISSANCE DRAMA SERIES

General Editor: Cyrus Hoy
Advisory Editor: G. E. Bentley

'TIS PITY SHE'S A WHORE

JOHN FORD

'Tis Pity She's a Whore

Edited by

N. W. BAWCUTT

UNIVERSITY OF NEBRASKA PRESS
LINCOLN AND LONDON

Copyright © 1966 by the University of Nebraska Press
All Rights Reserved
Library of Congress Catalog Card Number: 65–15339
International Standard Book Number 0-8032-5261-7

First printing: April, 1966
Most recent printing shown by first digit below:

10

MANUFACTURED IN THE UNITED STATES OF AMERICA

Regents Renaissance Drama Series

The purpose of the Regents Renaissance Drama Series is to provide soundly edited texts, in modern spelling, of the more significant plays of the Elizabethan, Jacobean, and Caroline theater. Each text in the series is based on a fresh collation of all sixteenth- and seventeenth-century editions. The textual notes, which appear above the line at the bottom of each page, record all substantive departures from the edition used as the copy-text. Variant substantive readings among sixteenth- and seventeenth-century editions are listed there as well. In cases where two or more of the old editions present widely divergent readings, a list of substantive variants in editions through the seventeenth century is given in an appendix. Editions after 1700 are referred to in the textual notes only when an emendation originating in some one of them is received into the text. Variants of accidentals (spelling, punctuation, capitalization) are not recorded in the notes. Contracted forms of characters' names are silently expanded in speech prefixes and stage directions, and, in the case of speech prefixes, are regularized. Additions to the stage directions of the copy-text are enclosed in brackets. Stage directions such as "within" or "aside" are enclosed in parentheses when they occur in the copy-text.

Spelling has been modernized along consciously conservative lines. "Murther" has become "murder," and "burthen," "burden," but within the limits of a modernized text, and with the following exceptions, the linguistic quality of the original has been carefully preserved. The variety of contracted forms (*'em, 'am, 'm, 'um, 'hem*) used in the drama of the period for the pronoun *them* are here regularly given as *'em*, and the alternation between *a'th'* and *o'th'* (for *on* or *of the*) is regularly reproduced as *o'th'*. The copy-text distinction between preterite endings in *-d* and *-ed* is preserved except where the elision of *e* occurs in the penultimate syllable; in such cases, the final syllable is contracted. Thus, where the old editions read "threat'ned," those of the present series read "threaten'd." Where, in the old editions, a contracted preterite in *-y'd* would yield *-i'd* in modern spelling (as in "try'd," "cry'd," "deny'd"), the word is here given in its full form (e.g., "tried," "cried," "denied").

Punctuation has been brought into accord with modern practices. The effort here has been to achieve a balance between the generally light pointing of the old editions, and a system of punctuation which, without overloading the text with exclamation marks, semicolons, and dashes, will make the often loosely flowing verse (and prose) of the original syntactically intelligible to the modern reader. Dashes are regularly used only to indicate interrupted speeches, or shifts of address within a single speech.

Explanatory notes, chiefly concerned with glossing obsolete words and phrases, are printed below the textual notes at the bottom of each page. References to stage directions in the notes follow the admirable system of the Revels editions, whereby stage directions are keyed, decimally, to the line of the text before or after which they occur. Thus, a note on 0.2 has reference to the second line of the stage direction at the beginning of the scene in question. A note on 115.1 has reference to the first line of the stage direction following line 115 of the text of the relevant scene.

CYRUS HOY

University of Rochester

Contents

Abbreviations

Dodsley	R. Dodsley, ed. *A Select Collection of Old Plays*. London, 1744.
Dyce	Alexander Dyce, ed. *The Works of John Ford*. London, 1869.
Gifford	William Gifford, ed. *The Dramatic Works of John Ford*. London, 1827.
McIlwraith	A. K. McIlwraith, ed. *Five Stuart Tragedies*. The World's Classics. Oxford, 1953.
OED	*Oxford English Dictionary*
Q	Quarto, 1633
Q uncorr.⎫ Q corr. ⎭	The uncorrected and corrected versions of the quarto text where there are variants caused by press-correction.
Reed	Isaac Reed, ed. *A Select Collection of Old Plays* (2nd edn.) London, 1780.
S.D.	stage direction
S.P.	speech prefix
Tilley	Morris Palmer Tilley. *A Dictionary of the Proverbs in England in the Sixteenth and Seventeenth Centuries*. Ann Arbor, 1950.
Weber	Henry Weber, ed. *The Dramatic Works of John Ford*. Edinburgh, 1811.

Introduction

DATE AND SOURCES

The title page of John Ford's *'Tis Pity She's a Whore*, published in 1633, states that it was "Acted by the Queenes Maiesties Seruants, at The Phoenix in Drury-Lane." This suggests that the first performance took place between 1626, when the Queen's company came into being, and 1633, the date of publication, but there is no certain evidence for a more precise date. In the dedication Ford describes the play as "these first fruits of my leisure," and some scholars have taken this to mean that it is his first independent play; but Ford merely seems to be saying that it is the first literary production of an unspecified period of leisure, which may have occurred at any time. As Gerald Bentley comments, there may have been some connection between the leisure and the "particular engagement" that Ford owed to Peterborough, but the form this engagement took has not yet been identified.[1] S. P. Sherman suggested that Ford was inspired to write his play by the case of Sir Giles Allington, who married the daughter of his half-sister, and was tried and severely punished for this offense in May, 1631.[2] If this was so it would help to date the play, but it is no more than speculation.

There is no record of a performance before the closing of the theaters in 1642, though *'Tis Pity She's a Whore* was included in a long list of plays which the Lord Chamberlain protected for William Beeston on August 10, 1639, by forbidding other companies to perform them. (William Beeston's father Christopher had been the manager of the Queen's company.)

The first Restoration revival is recorded by Pepys in his diary on September 9, 1661, at the Salisbury Court playhouse. He thought it "a simple play, and ill acted," but was pleased by a very pretty

---

[1] Gerald Bentley, *The Jacobean and Caroline Stage* (Oxford, 1942–1956), III, 463.

[2] S. P. Sherman, ed., *'Tis Pity She's a Whore and The Broken Heart* (Boston, 1915), p. xxxvi.

woman whom he luckily happened to sit by. Edward Browne saw the play at the King's Arms, Norwich, in 1662 or 1663.

The next revival was not until over two centuries later, when Maurice Maeterlinck's translated and abridged version was performed in Paris in 1894. The first revival of the English text took place in London in 1923, and in recent years there have been numerous performances by professional and amateur companies.

No definite source has yet been discovered for the plot of *'Tis Pity She's a Whore*. Scholars have drawn attention to various earlier treatments of the theme of brother and sister incest, but in none of them are the similarities so close as to put Ford's indebtedness beyond question. Among these analogues are Rosset's *Histoires Tragiques*, 1615, no. 5, derived from Pierre Matthieu's *Histoire de France et des Choses Memorables*, 1606; the fifth of the love-romances of Parthenios, retold in Thomas Heywood's *Gunaikeion*, 1624; and a play by the Italian dramatist Sperone Speroni, *Canace e Macareo*, 1546, based on the eleventh of Ovid's *Heroides*. From Spanish drama we might add a play roughly contemporary with Ford's, Tirso de Molina's *La Venganza de Tamar*. All these, however, are to be regarded as parallels rather than sources, and there are wide divergencies in the different authors' attitudes towards incest.

Ford clearly knew the work of his English predecessors, and critics have frequently noted the similarities between *'Tis Pity She's a Whore* and Shakespeare's *Romeo and Juliet*, with Giovanni, Annabella, Putana, and Friar Bonaventura as equivalents for Romeo, Juliet, the nurse, and Friar Lawrence. The death of Annabella (V.v) has been compared to the death of Desdemona (*Othello*, V.ii), and there may possibly be in the play a couple of faint verbal echoes of *Hamlet*. Ford had also read Marlowe, and one or two lines in *'Tis Pity She's a Whore* are reminiscent of *Tamburlaine* and *Dr. Faustus*. Finally, Bergetto is somewhat similar in character to the ward in Middleton's *Women Beware Women* (?1621), a play which also deals with the theme of incest.

THE PLAY

The central situation of *'Tis Pity She's a Whore* is an incestuous love between brother and sister, and it is hardly surprising that critics have differed widely in their interpretation of the exact meaning and significance of the play. Gerard Langbaine, writing in the seventeenth century, admired *'Tis Pity She's a Whore* but felt that Ford had portrayed incest too sympathetically:

> All that I can say is, that it equalls any of our Author's Plays; and were to be commended, did not the Author paint the incestuous Loue between *Giovanni*, and his sister *Annabella*, in too beautiful Colours.[3]

This was later echoed by Gifford:

> It is not easy to speak too favourably of the poetry of this play in the more impassioned passages; it is in truth too seductive for the subject, and flings a soft and soothing light over what, in its natural state, would glare with salutary and repulsive horror.[4]

Some twentieth-century critics have pushed this argument to an extreme, presenting Ford as a deliberate perverter of morality, a worshipper of the supreme value of love, which deserves to triumph over convention and morality.[5] This approach seems to be based on the rather rash assumption that Giovanni's attitudes (which are not always consistent) are to be identified with Ford's private attitudes, and it does not pay sufficient attention to the fact that a play must be interpreted by everything it contains and not merely by the speeches of a single character, no matter how important that character may be. Perhaps because of this, more recent critics have tended to see Ford as much more balanced, and less unorthodox, in his treatment of morality. Obviously the truth lies somewhere between two possible extremes of interpretation—Ford as apologist for immorality, a devotee of the religion of love, and Ford as stern moralist, showing by example that the wages of sin is death. There may even be evidence available for both of these views, and though this does not make the critic's job any easier, it should warn him not to oversimplify a difficult play.

Why, we might ask, did Ford choose incest as his central theme? One answer is that he needed to portray extreme situations in order to tempt the palate of an audience jaded by several decades of

[3] G. Langbaine, *An Account of the English Dramatick Poets* (Oxford, 1691), p. 222.

[4] William Gifford, ed., *The Dramatic Works of John Ford* (London, 1827), I, xxiv.

[5] A good example of this is Sherman's introduction to his edition.

theatrical sensationalism.[6] But this hardly seems a complete explanation. His motives in choosing incest need not have been crudely sensationalist; as Shelley remarked, after reading Calderon's *Los Cabellos de Absolon*:

> Incest is like many other *incorrect* things a very poetical circumstance. It may be the excess of love or of hate. It may be that defiance of everything for the sake of another which clothes itself in the glory of the highest heroism, or it may be that cynical rage which confounding the good and bad in existing opinions breaks through them for the purpose of rioting in selfishness and antipathy.[7]

In addition, Ford was obviously deeply interested in the brother and sister relationship, which he introduced into four of his other plays, and he may have felt that on this occasion he would explore the relationship in its most extreme form.

Several dramatists had, of course, used the theme of incest earlier than Ford—Tourneur, for example, in *The Revenger's Tragedy*, Beaumont and Fletcher in *A King and No King*, and Middleton in *Women Beware Women*—and it does seem true to say that Ford's treatment of the theme has less of the note of shocked horror and revulsion which is prominent in that of most of his predecessors. Ford appears to view the two lovers with a fair degree of sympathy and pity, though this does not necessarily mean, as we shall see, that he approves their love. (Even this, however, would be immoral to anyone who believed that incest must always be portrayed as vile and criminal, whatever the circumstances, but probably few modern critics would take such a rigorous attitude.) The two lovers are described in the play as highly gifted and attractive young people, whose love springs more from the intense admiration they feel for each other than from mere sensuality.[8] When Annabella sees Giovanni for the first time in the play, he strikes her as a "blessed shape/ Of some

6 H. J. Oliver, *The Problem of John Ford* (Melbourne, 1955), pp. 2–3.

7 Letter to Maria Gisborne, November 16, 1819 (*Letters* ed., F. L. Jones [Oxford, 1964], II, 154).

8 It might be argued as a weakness of the play that Ford, unlike Shakespeare in *Romeo and Juliet*, does not present his pair of lovers with sufficient creative richness for their attractiveness to come over fully to the audience; he relies too much on description of them, and this may explain why T. S. Eliot refuses to see the love between them as anything more than "purely carnal infatuation" (*Selected Essays* [London, 1932], p. 197).

celestial creature" (I.ii.126–127), and she describes him to Soranzo, in IV.iii, in similar terms. Giovanni emphasizes repeatedly that he loves his sister for her beauty, and in II.v he argues that this beauty is a sure indication both of Annabella's virtue and of the validity of their love, though it seems plain that the audience is intended to regard his arguments as ingenious sophistries. This is not the only indication that Ford could be critical of excessive worship of human beauty: in her repentance Annabella comes to see that

> Beauty that clothes the outside of the face
> Is cursed if it be not cloth'd with grace
>
> (V.i.12–13)

and there is an implied criticism of Giovanni in Soranzo's claim, perhaps hypocritical and unjustified, that he loved Annabella more for her virtues than her beauty, unlike her unknown lover (IV.iii. 122–129). In other words, though the motives which inspired the incestuous love are not entirely unworthy, they are not enough to justify it. All that can be claimed, as even Giovanni himself recognizes, is that this particular incestuous love is less offensive than such loves usually are:

> . . . if ever after-times should hear
> Of our fast-knit affections, though perhaps
> The laws of conscience and of civil use
> May justly blame us, yet when they but know
> Our loves, that love will wipe away that rigor
> Which would in other incests be abhorr'd.
>
> (V.v.68–73)

The tragedy of the two lovers is that they love deeply and are ideally suited to each other, but there is a barrier between them which makes a successful and permanent love impossible, and the play as a whole never suggests that this barrier could or should be removed.

The play's treatment of love in general makes it difficult to see Ford as an apostle of free love. All the love-affairs in the play end in disaster, including the comparatively innocent one between Bergetto and Philotis, and it would even be possible to read the play as a series of warnings against the destructive effects of passion. (Compare Richardetto's choric comment at IV.i.101–102, "Here's the end/ Of lust and pride" with his speech at V.vi.152–154.) There is considerable irony in the complacent and sentimental way in which Soranzo at the beginning of II.ii rewrites Sannazaro's pessimistic couplet on the nature of love, since his own subsequent experience shows the essential truth of it. When the play is seen in this light Richardetto's advice to Philotis to forsake the world and become a nun, in IV.ii, is not merely a clumsy plot-device to get rid of her, and such moralisings as

> All human worldly courses are uneven;
> No life is blessed but the way to Heaven,
> (IV.ii.20–21)

though completely conventional, are an essential part of the play's meaning, despite the fact that Richardetto is a rather dubious character and Philotis is amazingly docile by modern standards. All this suggests that human love is not by any means the supreme value in the moral world of the play.

There are several references to fate in *'Tis Pity She's a Whore*, and also in Ford's other plays, and some critics have interpreted this as implying that Ford is a fatalist whose characters are helplessly borne along by an inescapable destiny. Clearly Ford was interested in the effects of fate and destiny on the lives of human beings, but this is hardly enough to make him a fatalist in the sense just given. Critics do not seem to have realized how frequently Ford uses the word "Heaven" in *'Tis Pity She's a Whore* (over thirty times), and these allusions build up a clear picture of a divine agency intervening in human affairs.[9] The suggestion of divine intervention is most strongly felt, perhaps, in V.i, where the repentant Annabella, at the window of a room in which she is a prisoner, hopes to encounter someone who can take her letter to Giovanni. The Friar passes by, and is willing to act as her messenger, but this does not come about by chance:

> Lady, Heaven hath heard you,
> And hath by providence ordain'd that I
> Should be his minister for your behoof.
> (V.i.37–39)

---

[9] The evidence is too detailed to quote in full; compare, for example, I.i.67, 74, II.v.9, III.vi.34, and III.ix.68. Other phrases allude more or less directly to God himself (compare I.i.11, 44, II.v.64, IV.i.7, and IV.ii.8–9).

Annabella sees this as a mark of divine favor:

> Is Heaven so bountiful? Then I have found
> More favor than I hop'd.   (V.i.44–45)

The couplet with which she concludes the scene uses similar language:

> Thanks to the Heavens, who have prolong'd my breath
> To this good use: now I can welcome death.

There seems to be an implication that Annabella has been granted this favor because she wishes to put it to "good use" (though we are not told of the contents of the letter, it obviously urges Giovanni to repent).

But fate does not always work as the characters wish it to; Richardetto plans the destruction of Soranzo, and confidently announces:

> Thus shall the fates decree:
> By me Soranzo falls, that ruin'd me.
>   (II.iii.62–63)

But Soranzo does not fall, and by his clumsy plotting Richardetto succeeds only in bringing about the death of his prospective son-in-law Bergetto. (This, at any rate, is one way of looking at it; Grimaldi, the murderer of Bergetto by mistake, regards the killing of the wrong person as "merely chance," III.ix.48.) Giovanni makes more references to fate than anyone else in *'Tis Pity She's a Whore*, but his attitude is a special problem that may be deferred until his character in general is considered. Ford does not seem to have worked out a consistent and coherent theory of the relationship between fate and chance, and of the extent to which they are controlled by divine purposes, but his works do not give the impression that he saw man as the plaything of random and inexplicable forces. His little pamphlet, *A Line of Life* (1620), contains the argument that

> the fabricke of the globe of the earth would of necessitie runne to the confusion out of which it was first refined, if there were not a great and watchfull prouidence, to measure it in the just ballance of preseruing and sustayning . . . [10]

and *The Lover's Melancholy*, which may be his first independent play, and owes much of its atmosphere to Shakespeare's late romances, is

[10] John Ford, *Honour Triumphant and A Line of Life* (Shakespeare Society Publications, London, 1843), p. 49.

permeated with the sense of a benevolent destiny that helps man even when he tries to thwart it.

'*Tis Pity She's a Whore* is very much a tragedy of revenge, and the desire for revenge motivates most of the action of the play. In the early scenes Grimaldi, Hippolita, and Richardetto plot against Soranzo; in the later part of the play there is a kind of duel between Soranzo and Giovanni. Ford does not seem to sympathize with the desire for revenge; for the most part he portrays it as self-destructive, particularly in the case of Hippolita, and it is surely significant that in IV.ii Richardetto abandons his attempts at revenge because the signs of divine displeasure with Soranzo are becoming clearly apparent.[11]

Closely linked to the theme of revenge is the theme of justice. The other characters see Hippolita's death as a divine punishment ("Wonderful justice!" IV.i.88), and at the end of the play Donado regards the working-out of events as a "Strange miracle of justice" (V.vi.109). In the opening scene the Friar had already warned Giovanni that "Heaven is just" (I.i.67), and death would be the inevitable retribution for his sin, and in V.i Annabella admits that the Friar's warnings were right, that only the evil-minded refuse to acknowledge the justice of divine providence:

> But they who sleep in lethargies of lust
> Hug their confusion, making Heaven unjust,
> And so did I.   (V.i.28–30)

Human administration of justice, however, is not at all infallible, as is strikingly shown in the Cardinal's blatant disregard of it in III.ix, but even here Florio retains his faith that justice will eventually be done:

> Great men may do their wills, we must obey;
> But Heaven will judge them for't another day.
>   (III.ix.67–68)

One effect of this incident is to make it difficult to know how seriously we should take the Cardinal's pronouncements at the end of the play.

It may be useful to approach '*Tis Pity She's a Whore* from another direction and consider the leading characters individually in more detail. Three in particular have aroused critical discussion and controversy: these are Giovanni, Annabella, and the Friar.

---

[11] For fuller discussion of this aspect of the play see F. T. Bowers, *Elizabethan Revenge Tragedy 1587–1642* (Princeton, 1940), pp. 206–211.

Giovanni is first presented to us as the brilliant young student, a "miracle of wit," fresh from his university, and overconfident in his intellectual powers. The Friar has to warn him that he is no longer at the university, where "nice philosophy" can indulge harmlessly in unorthodox speculation, but in a real situation involving a choice of salvation or damnation. The Friar's description of the dangers of intellectual pride inevitably reminds us of Marlowe's *Dr. Faustus*:

> . . . wits that presum'd
> On wit too much, by striving how to prove
> There was no God, with foolish grounds of art,
> Discover'd first the nearest way to hell,
> And fill'd the world with devilish atheism.
>
> (I.i.4–8)

At this stage Giovanni is still tortured by the incompatibility between his love and traditional morality, but even in the first scene there is a hint of the overpoweringly obsessive nature of his love:

> It were more ease to stop the ocean
> From floats and ebbs than to dissuade my vows.
>
> (I.i.64–65)

He is ready to obey the Friar's recommendations, but pays steadily less attention to the Friar as the play proceeds.

In the early scenes Giovanni uses various arguments to defend his love.[12] One is a rather debased version of the neoplatonic worship of beauty found in Spenser's *An Hymn in Honour of Beauty* or Book IV of Castiglione's *The Courtier*. Another is that nearness of blood necessarily involves a greater community of feeling. A third is that he is fated to love Annabella, and cannot escape his destiny. (This in a sense is true, since he is determined to persist in his love, but it is his own view of his predicament and should not be taken as Ford's private opinion.) But when all his ideas are put together they hardly

---

[12] To be seen in perspective, Giovanni's arguments should be compared with the speech in defense of incest by Rhegius in Chettle's *Piers Plainness*, 1595 (ed. James Winny, *The Descent of Euphues* [Cambridge, 1957], pp. 154–155) or such dramatic treatments as Tourneur's *The Atheist's Tragedy*, IV.iii, Beaumont and Fletcher's *A King and No King*, IV.iv, and Massinger's *The Unnatural Combat*, V.ii. See also Donne, *The Progress of the Soul*, ll. 191–203. One source for some of the ideas expressed in these works is Myrrha's speech in Ovid's *Metamorphoses*, X, 320–355.

amount to a coherent and consistent philosophy; indeed, a harsh critic might call them a queer muddle of inconsistencies, and it is hard to believe that Ford intended Giovanni to embody any particular philosophical attitude. Giovanni's arguments are desperate rationalizations, sometimes ingenious but unconvincing, and their main purpose is surely to show us the way his mind works under the stress of his love.

It could be said that Giovanni becomes increasingly detached from reality as the play proceeds. Anything that stands in the way of his love is discarded or ignored: religion forbids an incestuous love, so he becomes an atheist, and when he is presented with Annabella's letter (in V.iii), which strikes at the root of his moral position, he brushes it aside by arguing that it is forged. The temporary success of his love induces in him a kind of euphoria in which he believes that, far from being driven by fate, he is in fact the controller of fate (see III.ii.20). This megalomania persists into the last scene of the play (" . . . in my fists I bear the twists of life," V.vi.72), but there is a note of pathetic disillusionment when he realises the truth (V.vi.81–84).

In V.v Giovanni murders Annabella, and though this act could have been inspired by a selfish resentment that she has been taken from him, it is also a fulfilment of their mutual vow ("love me or kill me") ; as the Friar had warned (I.i.59), death is the inevitable outcome of their love. The murder of Soranzo is less excusable, and shows Giovanni, in Shelley's phrase, "rioting in selfishness and antipathy."

Annabella is a more thoughtful and sensitive person than her brother. She loves deeply, but makes no attempt to justify her love by sophistries, and pays more attention than Giovanni to the opinions and feelings of others. She is unselfishly concerned for her brother, refusing to betray him even at the cost of her life, and when she repents of her sin she tries hard to persuade him to repent.

However, she has not always been seen in such a favorable light. Gifford rebuked Weber for describing Annabella as "interesting for everything which can render a female mind amiable," and said that "her repentance is of a very questionable nature,"[13] and Eliot regards her as "pliant, vacillating, and negative . . . virtually a moral defective."[14] This plainly is too severe; there is no reason to doubt that Annabella's repentance at the end of the play is sincere and genuine, though there is a problem involved in the repentance induced by the

[13] Gifford, I, xxiv–xxv.
[14] Eliot, *op. cit.*, p. 198.

Friar's vivid description of the torments of hell in III.vi. In what mood does she marry Soranzo, and is she unfaithful to him, as is suggested by V.iii.4–11? The play does not give all the evidence needed for an answer.[15] Possibly Annabella intended to be faithful to Soranzo, but his violent anger at the discovery of her pregnancy (in some ways understandable enough) is so extreme that she realizes that the marriage has no chance of success, and deliberately taunts him in the hope that he will be provoked into killing her. She meets Giovanni only once, at the end of IV.iii, in the time between her marriage and her death-scene, but Ford does not portray this meeting on the stage. We next see her, in V.i, as repentant for her sin ("love" is now "lust"), but anxious to help her brother, even to the extent of taking over all the guilt for their relationship. Her last major speech (V.v.16–29) is grave and earnest, yet affectionate, and this is probably the dominant impression of her that Ford wanted to leave in our minds.

Friar Bonaventura has usually been discussed in a distinctly unfavorable manner, and three main charges have been made against him. In the first place, he fails to provide intellectually convincing arguments to answer those put forward by Giovanni in the early part of the play; secondly, he urges Annabella to marry Soranzo, knowing that she is already pregnant; and finally, he goes away in what some critics feel is a rather cowardly fashion when he sees that he is powerless to influence events.

Some defense is possible against these accusations. It is hard to know what arguments could have been successfully used to counter Giovanni's mood at the beginning of the play. (What would those who blame the Friar have said in his position?) His advocacy of the marriage seems dishonest to many critics, and it is certainly foolish in view of Soranzo's character (which the Friar may not necessarily know about), but his main motive is to save the souls of the lovers, and he may regard the marriage solely as a means to this end. He came to Parma because of his affection for Giovanni, and it seems hard to blame him for going away when he realizes that Giovanni completely disregards his advice. Whatever criticisms may be made of the Friar, the impression still remains that Ford intended him as an admirable representative of orthodox morality (in contrast to the Cardinal), and the other characters in the play venerate him.

The most striking incident in the final scene is Giovanni's entry

[15] There is one problem of chronology; V.ii appears to follow on directly from IV.iii, but V.i must take place some time after IV.iii.

with the heart of Annabella on his dagger. This has been viewed as sensationalism, but also as a piece of obscure yet powerful symbolism; for some critics it represents the triumph of love, for others, tragic waste and destruction.[16] It would certainly be wise to regard the incident as emblematic rather than realistic, but it is not easy to limit it to any single meaning, and in this respect it may legitimately stand as a symbol of the play as a whole. Throughout Ford portrays events which, barely narrated, could easily be regarded as crudely sensationalist, but in his hands they take on difficult and disturbing meanings that are not easily defined.

THE TEXT

'Tis Pity She's a Whore was first published in 1633, in quarto, without entry in the Stationers' Register, and was printed by Nicholas Okes for Richard Collins. Ford's dedication shows that he authorized the publication, and the general cleanness of the text suggests that he supplied a fair copy to the printer. The compositor was careless at times and perhaps inexperienced, and made a number of minor errors: he misattributes speeches, duplicates words and phrases, and occasionally omits words. There may possibly have been a second compositor for gatherings H to K (from IV.iii.15 onwards), since there are fewer mistakes of the kind described above, and fresh mistakes of a different kind, and a more frequent use of italic type. For this edition sixteen copies in the British Isles were collated, and the collation revealed nearly forty press-variants, many of which were unnoticed by earlier editors. They do not radically alter the text, but they throw light on the compositors' characteristics, and help the editor to emend more confidently. (A selection of the more interesting press-variants is given in the textual notes.) The play was first reprinted by Dodsley in 1744. There were several editions in the nineteenth century, and in the past thirty years the play has frequently been reprinted in anthologies of drama.

N. W. BAWCUTT

University of Liverpool

[16] It is to some extent prepared for earlier in the play; compare I.ii.205–208 and IV.iii.53–54.

'TIS PITY SHE'S A WHORE

TO MY FRIEND THE AUTHOR

With admiration I beheld this Whore
Adorn'd with beauty such as might restore
(If ever being as thy muse hath fam'd)
Her Giovanni, in his love unblam'd:
The ready Graces lent their willing aid,
Pallas herself now play'd the chambermaid,
And help'd to put her dressings on. Secure
Rest thou that thy name herein shall endure
To th' end of age; and Annabella be
Gloriously fair, even in her infamy.

THOMAS ELLICE

Thomas Ellice] Possibly a relative of the Robert Ellice of Gray's Inn to whom Ford dedicated *The Lover's Melancholy*. Both men wrote complimentary poems to D'Avenant's *Albovine* (1629).

TO THE TRULY NOBLE
JOHN, EARL OF PETERBOROUGH, LORD
MORDAUNT, BARON OF TURVEY

My Lord,

Where a truth of merit hath a general warrant, there   5
love is but a debt, acknowledgment a justice. Greatness
cannot often claim virtue by inheritance; yet, in this, yours
appears most eminent, for that you are not more rightly
heir to your fortunes than glory shall be to your memory.
Sweetness of disposition ennobles a freedom of birth; in   10
both, your lawful interest adds honor to your own name
and mercy to my presumption. Your noble allowance of
these first fruits of my leisure in the action emboldens my
confidence of your as noble construction in this presentment;
especially since my service must ever owe particular duty to 15
your favors by a particular engagement. The gravity of the
subject may easily excuse the lightness of the title, otherwise
I had been a severe judge against mine own guilt. Princes
have vouchsaf'd grace to trifles offer'd from a purity of
devotion; your lordship may likewise please to admit into   20
your good opinion, with these weak endeavors, the constancy
of affection from the sincere lover of your deserts in honor,

JOHN FORD

2–3. John Mordaunt (1599–1643) was created first Earl of Peterborough
in 1628.

12. *allowance*] approval.

13. *in the action*] when performed on the stage.

14. *construction*] interpretation, opinion.

14. *in this presentment*] in print.

The Actors' Names

BONAVENTURA, *a friar*
A CARDINAL, *nuncio to the Pope*
SORANZO, *a nobleman*
FLORIO, *a citizen of Parma*
DONADO, *another citizen*
GRIMALDI, *a Roman gentleman*
GIOVANNI, *son to Florio*
BERGETTO, *nephew to Donado*
RICHARDETTO, *a suppos'd physician*
VASQUES, *servant to Soranzo*
POGGIO, *servant to Bergetto*
BANDITTI, [OFFICERS, ATTENDANTS, &c.]

Women

ANNABELLA, *daughter to Florio*
HIPPOLITA, *wife to Richardetto*
PHILOTIS, *his niece*
PUTANA, *tut'ress to Annabella*
[LADIES]

The Scene: *Parma*

'Tis Pity She's a Whore

Enter Friar *and* Giovanni.

FRIAR.

    Dispute no more in this, for know, young man,
    These are no school-points; nice philosophy
    May tolerate unlikely arguments,
    But Heaven admits no jest: wits that presum'd
    On wit too much, by striving how to prove   5
    There was no God, with foolish grounds of art,
    Discover'd first the nearest way to hell,
    And fill'd the world with devilish atheism.
    Such questions, youth, are fond; for better 'tis
    To bless the sun than reason why it shines,   10
    Yet He thou talk'st of is above the sun.
    No more; I may not hear it.

GIOVANNI.   Gentle father,
    To you I have unclasp'd my burdened soul,
    Emptied the storehouse of my thoughts and heart,
    Made myself poor of secrets; have not left   15
    Another word untold, which hath not spoke
    All what I ever durst or think or know;
    And yet is here the comfort I shall have,
    Must I not do what all men else may, love?

FRIAR.

    Yes, you may love, fair son.

GIOVANNI.   Must I not praise   20
    That beauty which, if fram'd anew, the gods
    Would make a god of, if they had it there,
    And kneel to it, as I do kneel to them?

---

2. *school-points*] topics for academic debate.
6. *art*] learning.
9. *fond*] foolish.

FRIAR.
>   Why, foolish madman—
GIOVANNI.   Shall a peevish sound,
>   A customary form, from man to man,   25
>   Of brother and of sister, be a bar
>   'Twixt my perpetual happiness and me?
>   Say that we had one father, say one womb
>   (Curse to my joys) gave both us life and birth;
>   Are we not therefore each to other bound   30
>   So much the more by nature, by the links
>   Of blood, of reason—nay, if you will have't,
>   Even of religion—to be ever one,
>   One soul, one flesh, one love, one heart, one all?
FRIAR.
>   Have done, unhappy youth, for thou art lost.   35
GIOVANNI.
>   Shall then, for that I am her brother born,
>   My joys be ever banish'd from her bed?
>   No, father; in your eyes I see the change
>   Of pity and compassion; from your age,
>   As from a sacred oracle, distils   40
>   The life of counsel: tell me, holy man,
>   What cure shall give me ease in these extremes.
FRIAR.
>   Repentance, son, and sorrow for this sin:
>   For thou hast mov'd a Majesty above
>   With thy unranged-almost blasphemy.   45
GIOVANNI.
>   O do not speak of that, dear confessor!
FRIAR.
>   Art thou, my son, that miracle of wit
>   Who once, within these three months, wert esteem'd
>   A wonder of thine age, throughout Bononia?
>   How did the University applaud   50
>   Thy government, behavior, learning, speech,

---

25. *customary form*] mere convention, formality.
45. *unranged*] probably meaning "wildly disordered".
49. *Bononia*] Bologna, famous for its university.
51. *government*] good conduct, discretion.

Sweetness, and all that could make up a man!
I was proud of my tutelage, and chose
Rather to leave my books than part with thee.
I did so: but the fruits of all my hopes   55
Are lost in thee, as thou art in thyself.
O, Giovanni, hast thou left the schools
Of knowledge to converse with lust and death?
For death waits on thy lust. Look through the world,
And thou shalt see a thousand faces shine   60
More glorious than this idol thou ador'st:
Leave her, and take thy choice, 'tis much less sin,
Though in such games as those they lose that win.

GIOVANNI.
It were more ease to stop the ocean
From floats and ebbs than to dissuade my vows.   65

FRIAR.
Then I have done, and in thy wilful flames
Already see thy ruin; Heaven is just.
Yet hear my counsel.

GIOVANNI.   As a voice of life.

FRIAR.
Hie to thy father's house, there lock thee fast
Alone within thy chamber, then fall down   70
On both thy knees, and grovel on the ground:
Cry to thy heart, wash every word thou utter'st
In tears, and (if't be possible) of blood:
Beg Heaven to cleanse the leprosy of lust
That rots thy soul, acknowledge what thou art,   75
A wretch, a worm, a nothing: weep, sigh, pray
Three times a day, and three times every night.
For seven days' space do this, then if thou find'st
No change in thy desires, return to me:
I'll think on remedy. Pray for thyself   80
At home, whilst I pray for thee here. —Away,
My blessing with thee, we have need to pray.

---

57. *Giovanni*] to be pronounced with four syllables, not three as in Italian.
65. *floats*] flows.
65. *vows*] wishes, prayers.

GIOVANNI.

    All this I'll do, to free me from the rod

    Of vengeance; else I'll swear my fate's my god.   *Exeunt.*

[I.ii]   *Enter* Grimaldi *and* Vasques *ready to fight.*

VASQUES.

    Come, sir, stand to your tackling; if you prove craven, I'll

    make you run quickly.

GRIMALDI.

    Thou art no equal match for me.

VASQUES.

    Indeed I never went to the wars to bring home news,

    nor cannot play the mountebank for a meal's meat, and   5

    swear I got my wounds in the field. See you these grey hairs?

    They'll not flinch for a bloody nose. Wilt thou to this gear?

GRIMALDI.

    Why, slave, think'st thou I'll balance my reputation with

    a cast-suit? Call thy master, he shall know that I dare—

VASQUES.

    Scold like a cot-quean, that's your profession. Thou poor   10

    shadow of a soldier, I will make thee know my master keeps

    servants thy betters in quality and performance. Com'st thou

    to fight or prate?

GRIMALDI.

    Neither, with thee. I am a Roman and a gentleman, one that

    have got mine honor with expense of blood.   15

VASQUES.

    You are a lying coward and a fool; fight, or by these hilts

    I'll kill thee. —Brave my lord! You'll fight?

14–15.] *Weber*; Neither . . . thee./ I
. . . got/ Mine . . . blood. *Q.*

---

    1. *tackling*] weapons.

    3. *equal*] socially equal; Grimaldi will not demean himself by fighting a
servant.

    7. *gear*] business (of fighting).

    9. *cast-suit*] servant wearing his master's cast-off clothing.

    10. *cot-quean*] a man with too much interest in domestic matters; hence,
effeminate and shrill.

    17. *Brave my lord!*] "Do you dare to challenge my master?"

GRIMALDI.

    Provoke me not, for if thou dost—

VASQUES.

    Have at you!

                    They fight, Grimaldi *hath the worst.*

         Enter Florio, Donado, Soranzo.

FLORIO.

    What mean these sudden broils so near my doors?   20
    Have you not other places but my house
    To vent the spleen of your disordered bloods?
    Must I be haunted still with such unrest
    As not to eat or sleep in peace at home?
    Is this your love, Grimaldi? Fie, 'tis naught.   25

DONADO.

    And Vasques, I may tell thee, 'tis not well
    To broach these quarrels; you are ever forward
    In seconding contentions.

         Enter above Annabella *and* Putana.

FLORIO.   What's the ground?

SORANZO.

    That, with your patience, signors, I'll resolve:
    This gentleman, whom fame reports a soldier,   30
    (For else I know not) rivals me in love
    To Signor Florio's daughter, to whose ears
    He still prefers his suit, to my disgrace,
    Thinking the way to recommend himself
    Is to disparage me in his report.   35
    But know, Grimaldi, though, may be, thou art
    My equal in thy blood, yet this bewrays
    A lowness in thy mind which, wert thou noble,
    Thou wouldst as much disdain as I do thee

---

20. mean] *Q corr.;* meaned *Q
uncorr.*

---

28. S.D. *above*] on the upper stage.
37. *bewrays*] betrays, reveals.

For this unworthiness; and on this ground   40
I will'd my servant to correct his tongue,
Holding a man so base no match for me.

VASQUES.

And had not your sudden coming prevented us, I had let
my gentleman blood under the gills; I should have worm'd
you, sir, for running mad.   45

GRIMALDI.

I'll be reveng'd, Soranzo.

VASQUES.

On a dish of warm broth to stay your stomach—do, honest
innocence, do; spoon-meat is a wholesomer diet than a
Spanish blade.

GRIMALDI.

Remember this!   50

SORANZO.

I fear thee not, Grimaldi.   *Exit* Grimaldi.

FLORIO.

My Lord Soranzo, this is strange to me,
Why you should storm, having my word engag'd:
Owing her heart, what need you doubt her ear?
Losers may talk by law of any game.   55

VASQUES.

Yet the villainy of words, Signor Florio, may be such as
would make any unspleen'd dove choleric. Blame not my
lord in this.

FLORIO.

Be you more silent.
I would not for my wealth my daughter's love   60
Should cause the spilling of one drop of blood.
Vasques, put up, let's end this fray in wine.

            Exeunt [Florio, Donado, Soranzo *and* Vasques].

41. his] *Dodsley;* this *Q*.   56–58.] *Weber;* Yet ... such/ As
43. had not] *Dodsley;* had *Q*.   ... choleric./ Blame ... this. *Q*.
56. villainy] *Dodsley;* villaine *Q*.

---

44. *worm'd*] "Worming" was an operation performed on dogs to prevent
madness.
48. *innocence*] fool.
54. *Owing*] owning.
57. *unspleen'd*] lacking spleen, not easily angered.
62. *put up*] sheathe your sword.

PUTANA.

>How like you this, child? Here's threat'ning, challenging,
quarreling, and fighting, on every side, and all is for your
sake; you had need look to yourself, charge, you'll be   65
stol'n away sleeping else shortly.

ANNABELLA.

>But tut'ress, such a life gives no content
To me, my thoughts are fix'd on other ends;
Would you would leave me.

PUTANA.

>Leave you? No marvel else. Leave me no leaving, charge;   70
this is love outright. Indeed I blame you not, you have choice
fit for the best lady in Italy.

ANNABELLA.

>Pray do not talk so much.

PUTANA.

>Take the worst with the best, there's Grimaldi the soldier,
a very well-timber'd fellow: they say he is a Roman,   75
nephew to the Duke Montferrato, they say he did good
service in the wars against the Milanese, but 'faith, charge,
I do not like him, an't be for nothing but for being a soldier;
not one amongst twenty of your skirmishing captains but
have some privy maim or other that mars their standing   80
upright. I like him the worse, he crinkles so much in the
hams; though he might serve if there were no more men,
yet he's not the man I would choose.

ANNABELLA.

>Fie, how thou prat'st.

PUTANA.

>As I am a very woman, I like Signor Soranzo well; he is   85
wise, and what is more, rich; and what is more than that,
kind, and what is more than all this, a nobleman; such a
one, were I the fair Annabella myself, I would wish and
pray for. Then he is bountiful; besides, he is handsome, and

70–72.] *Dodsley;* Leave . . . charge;/   78. an't] *Weber;* and *Q.*
This . . . have/ Choice . . . Italy. *Q.*   79. not one] *Dodsley;* one *Q.*

---

75. *well-timber'd*] sturdy, well-built.
80–81. *standing upright*] implying that their wounds have rendered them
impotent.

by my troth, I think wholesome (and that's news in a gallant   90
of three and twenty); liberal, that I know; loving, that you
know; and a man sure, else he could never ha' purchas'd
such a good name with Hippolita, the lusty widow, in her
husband's lifetime: and 'twere but for that report, sweetheart, would 'a were thine. Commend a man for his   95
qualities, but take a husband as he is a plain-sufficient,
naked man: such a one is for your bed, and such a one is
Signor Soranzo, my life for't.

ANNABELLA.

Sure the woman took her morning's draught too soon.

Enter Bergetto *and* Poggio.

PUTANA.

But look, sweetheart, look what thing comes now: here's 100
another of your ciphers to fill up the number. O brave
old ape in a silken coat! Observe.

BERGETTO.

Didst thou think, Poggio, that I would spoil my new
clothes, and leave my dinner, to fight?

POGGIO.

No, sir, I did not take you for so arrant a baby.   105

BERGETTO.

I am wiser than so: for I hope, Poggio, thou never heardst
of an elder brother that was a coxcomb. Didst, Poggio?

POGGIO.

Never indeed, sir, as long as they had either land or money
left them to inherit.

BERGETTO.

Is it possible, Poggio? O monstrous! Why, I'll undertake 110
with a handful of silver to buy a headful of wit at any time;
but sirrah, I have another purchase in hand, I shall have the

---

100–102.] *Weber;* But ... now:/   106–107.]   *Dodsley;*   I ... thou/
Here's ... number./O ... observe. *Q*.   Never ... coxcomb./ Didst, Pog-
103–104.] *Dodsley;* Didst ... my/   gio? *Q*.
New ... fight? *Q*.

---

90. *wholesome*] healthy, not diseased.
91. *liberal*] generous with money (to Putana).
94. *report*] rumor, gossip.

wench, mine uncle says. I will but wash my face, and shift
socks, and then have at her i'faith! Mark my pace, Poggio.

                                                    [*Walks affectedly.*]
POGGIO.

Sir—[*Aside.*] I have seen an ass and a mule trot the   115
Spanish pavin with a better grace, I know not how often.

                                    Exeunt [Bergetto *and* Poggio].
ANNABELLA.

This idiot haunts me too.

PUTANA.

Ay, ay, he needs no description; the rich magnifico that is
below with your father, charge, Signor Donado his uncle,
for that he means to make this his cousin a golden calf,   120
thinks that you will be a right Israelite and fall down to him
presently: but I hope I have tutor'd you better. They say a
fool's bauble is a lady's playfellow, yet you having wealth
enough, you need not cast upon the dearth of flesh at any
rate: hang him, innocent!   125

                            Enter Giovanni.
ANNABELLA.

But see, Putana, see: what blessed shape
Of some celestial creature now appears?
What man is he, that with such sad aspect
Walks careless of himself?

PUTANA.   Where?

ANNABELLA.   Look below.

PUTANA.

O, 'tis your brother, sweet.

ANNABELLA.   Ha!

PUTANA.   'Tis your brother.   130

ANNABELLA.

Sure 'tis not he: this is some woeful thing
Wrapp'd up in grief, some shadow of a man.

---

116. *pavin*] pavanne, a stately dance.
118. *magnifico*] person in authority, magistrate.
120. *golden calf*] see Exodus, chapter 32.
123. *bauble*] stick or truncheon (but with an indecent implication).
123–125. *yet you . . . rate*] Since Annabella is wealthy, she need not gamble
recklessly ("cast . . . at any rate") and accept Bergetto as a husband on the
assumption that there will be a shortage of suitors ("dearth of flesh").
125.1. *Enter*] on the main stage below.

Alas, he beats his breast, and wipes his eyes
Drown'd all in tears: methinks I hear him sigh.
Let's down, Putana, and partake the cause;   135
I know my brother, in the love he bears me,
Will not deny me partage in his sadness.
[*Aside.*] My soul is full of heaviness and fear.

                                        Exit [*with* Putana].

GIOVANNI.

Lost, I am lost: my fates have doom'd my death.
The more I strive, I love; the more I love,   140
The less I hope: I see my ruin certain.
What judgment or endeavors could apply
To my incurable and restless wounds
I throughly have examin'd, but in vain:
O that it were not in religion sin   145
To make our love a god and worship it!
I have even wearied Heaven with prayers, dried up
The spring of my continual tears, even starv'd
My veins with daily fasts: what wit or art
Could counsel, I have practic'd; but alas,   150
I find all these but dreams and old men's tales
To fright unsteady youth; I'm still the same.
Or I must speak, or burst; 'tis not, I know,
My lust, but 'tis my fate that leads me on.
Keep fear and low faint-hearted shame with slaves;   155
I'll tell her that I love her, though my heart
Were rated at the price of that attempt.
O me! She comes.

                Enter Annabella *and* Putana.

ANNABELLA.   Brother!
GIOVANNI [*aside*].   If such a thing
As courage dwell in men, ye heavenly powers,
Now double all that virtue in my tongue.   160

---

137. *partage*] a part or share.
138.] Some editors unnecessarily begin a new scene here. Annabella and
Putana descend from the upper to the main stage while Giovanni speaks
his soliloquy.
144. *throughly*] thoroughly.
155. *Keep*] live, dwell.

ANNABELLA.

Why, brother, will you not speak to me?

GIOVANNI.

Yes; how d'ee, sister?

ANNABELLA.

Howsoever I am, methinks you are not well.

PUTANA.

Bless us, why are you so sad, sir?

GIOVANNI.

Let me entreat you, leave us a while, Putana. Sister,   165
I would be private with you.

ANNABELLA.

Withdraw, Putana.

PUTANA.

I will. [*Aside.*] If this were any other company for her, I
should think my absence an office of some credit; but I
will leave them together.   *Exit* Putana. 170

GIOVANNI.

Come, sister, lend your hand, let's walk together.
I hope you need not blush to walk with me;
Here's none but you and I.

ANNABELLA.

How's this?

GIOVANNI.

Faith, I mean no harm.   175

ANNABELLA.

Harm?

GIOVANNI.

No, good faith; how is't with 'ee?

ANNABELLA [*aside*].

I trust he be not frantic. [*To him.*] I am very well, brother.

GIOVANNI.

Trust me, but I am sick, I fear so sick
'Twill cost my life.   180

ANNABELLA.

Mercy forbid it! 'Tis not so, I hope.

165–166.] *this edn.;* Let . . . Putana./
Sister . . . you. *Q.*

---

169. *of some credit*] deserving payment (as a bawd).
178. *frantic*] mad.

GIOVANNI.
     I think you love me, sister.

ANNABELLA.
     Yes, you know I do.

GIOVANNI.
     I know't indeed. —Y'are very fair.

ANNABELLA.
     Nay then, I see you have a merry sickness.   185

GIOVANNI.
     That's as it proves. The poets feign, I read,
     That Juno for her forehead did exceed
     All other goddesses: but I durst swear
     Your forehead exceeds hers, as hers did theirs.

ANNABELLA.
     Troth, this is pretty!

GIOVANNI.   Such a pair of stars   190
     As are thine eyes would, like Promethean fire,
     If gently glanc'd, give life to senseless stones.

ANNABELLA.
     Fie upon 'ee!

GIOVANNI.
     The lily and the rose, most sweetly strange,
     Upon your dimpled cheeks do strive for change.   195
     Such lips would tempt a saint; such hands as those
     Would make an anchorite lascivious.

ANNABELLA.
     D'ee mock me or flatter me?

GIOVANNI.
     If you would see a beauty more exact
     Than art can counterfeit or nature frame,   200
     Look in your glass and there behold your own.

ANNABELLA.
     O you are a trim youth!

GIOVANNI.
     Here.   *Offers his dagger to her.*

---

186. The] *Dodsley;* They *Q.*

---

191. *Promethean fire*] In Greek mythology Prometheus first brought fire
to men by stealing it from Heaven.

ANNABELLA.
What to do?
GIOVANNI.
—And here's my breast, strike home. 205
Rip up my bosom, there thou shalt behold
A heart in which is writ the truth I speak.
Why stand 'ee?
ANNABELLA.   Are you earnest?
GIOVANNI.   Yes, most earnest.
You cannot love?
ANNABELLA.   Whom?
GIOVANNI.   Me. My tortur'd soul
Hath felt affliction in the heat of death. 210
O Annabella, I am quite undone:
The love of thee, my sister, and the view
Of thy immortal beauty hath untun'd
All harmony both of my rest and life.
Why d'ee not strike?
ANNABELLA.   Forbid it, my just fears! 215
If this be true, 'twere fitter I were dead.
GIOVANNI.
True, Annabella; 'tis no time to jest.
I have too long suppress'd the hidden flames
That almost have consum'd me; I have spent
Many a silent night in sighs and groans, 220
Ran over all my thoughts, despis'd my fate,
Reason'd against the reasons of my love,
Done all that smooth-cheek'd virtue could advise,
But found all bootless; 'tis my destiny
That you must either love, or I must die. 225
ANNABELLA.
Comes this in sadness from you?
GIOVANNI.   Let some mischief
Befall me soon, if I dissemble aught.
ANNABELLA.
You are my brother Giovanni.

205. strike] *Dodsley;* strick *Q.*   223.   smooth-cheek'd] *Dodsley;*
                                            smooth'd-cheek *Q.*

224. *bootless*] useless.   226. *in sadness*] seriously, sincerely.

GIOVANNI.   You
    My sister Annabella; I know this:
    And could afford you instance why to love   230
    So much the more for this; to which intent
    Wise nature first in your creation meant
    To make you mine; else't had been sin and foul
    To share one beauty to a double soul.
    Nearness in birth or blood doth but persuade   235
    A nearer nearness in affection.
    I have ask'd counsel of the holy church,
    Who tells me I may love you, and 'tis just
    That since I may, I should; and will, yes, will:
    Must I now live, or die?

ANNABELLA.   Live: thou hast won   240
    The field, and never fought; what thou hast urg'd
    My captive heart had long ago resolv'd.
    I blush to tell thee—but I'll tell thee now—
    For every sigh that thou hast spent for me
    I have sigh'd ten; for every tear shed twenty: 245
    And not so much for that I lov'd, as that
    I durst not say I lov'd, nor scarcely think it.

GIOVANNI.
    Let not this music be a dream, ye gods,
    For pity's sake, I beg 'ee!

ANNABELLA.   On my knees,   *She kneels.*
    Brother, even by our mother's dust, I charge you,   250
    Do not betray me to your mirth or hate,
    Love me or kill me, brother.

GIOVANNI.   On my knees.   *He kneels.*
    Sister, even by my mother's dust, I charge you,
    Do not betray me to your mirth or hate,
    Love me or kill me, sister.   255

ANNABELLA.
    You mean good sooth then?

GIOVANNI.   In good troth I do,
    And so do you, I hope: say, I'm in earnest.

---

256. *sooth*] truth.

ANNABELLA.

I'll swear't, I.

GIOVANNI.   And I, and by this kiss,   *Kisses her.*

(Once more, yet once more; now let's rise by this),   [*They rise.*]

I would not change this minute for Elysium.   260

What must we now do?

ANNABELLA.   What you will.

GIOVANNI.   Come then,

After so many tears as we have wept,

Let's learn to court in smiles, to kiss, and sleep.

Exeunt.

[I.iii]   *Enter* Florio *and* Donado.

FLORIO.

Signor Donado, you have said enough,

I understand you; but would have you know

I will not force my daughter 'gainst her will.

You see I have but two, a son and her;

And he is so devoted to his book,   5

As I must tell you true, I doubt his health:

Should he miscarry, all my hopes rely

Upon my girl; as for worldly fortune,

I am, I thank my stars, blest with enough.

My care is how to match her to her liking: 10

I would not have her marry wealth, but love,

And if she like your nephew, let him have her,

Here's all that I can say.

DONADO.   Sir, you say well,

Like a true father, and for my part, I,

If the young folks can like ('twixt you and me),   15

Will promise to assure my nephew presently

Three thousand florins yearly during life,

And after I am dead, my whole estate.

---

258. swear't, I] *Gifford;* swear't and
I *Q.*

[I.iii]
6. *doubt*] worry about.

FLORIO.

    'Tis a fair proffer, sir; meantime your nephew
    Shall have free passage to commence his suit: 20
    If he can thrive, he shall have my consent.
    So for this time I'll leave you, signor.   *Exit.*

DONADO.   Well,

    Here's hope yet, if my nephew would have wit:
    But he is such another dunce, I fear
    He'll never win the wench. When I was young   25
    I could have done't, i'faith, and so shall he
    If he will learn of me; and in good time
    He comes himself.

                    Enter Bergetto *and* Poggio.

    How now, Bergetto, whither away so fast?

BERGETTO.

    O uncle, I have heard the strangest news that ever came   30
    out of the mint, have I not, Poggio?

POGGIO.

    Yes indeed, sir.

DONADO.

    What news, Bergetto?

BERGETTO.

    Why, look ye, uncle, my barber told me just now that
    there is a fellow come to town who undertakes to make a   35
    mill go without the mortal help of any water or wind,
    only with sand-bags: and this fellow hath a strange horse,
    a most excellent beast, I'll assure you, uncle (my barber
    says), whose head, to the wonder of all Christian people,
    stands just behind where his tail is; is't not true, Poggio?   40

POGGIO.

    So the barber swore, forsooth.

DONADO.

    And you are running thither?

BERGETTO.

    Ay forsooth, uncle.

DONADO.

    Wilt thou be a fool still? Come, sir, you shall not go: you

29. How . . . fast?] *Assigned to Don-*   42. thither] *Gifford;* hither *Q*.
ado by Weber; to Poggio in Q.

have more mind of a puppet-play than on the business I   45
told ye; why, thou great baby, wilt never have wit, wilt
make thyself a may-game to all the world?

POGGIO.

Answer for yourself, master.

BERGETTO.

Why, uncle, should I sit at home still, and not go abroad
to see fashions like other gallants?   50

DONADO.

To see hobby-horses! What wise talk, I pray, had you with
Annabella, when you were at Signor Florio's house?

BERGETTO.

O, the wench! Uds sa' me, uncle, I tickled her with a rare
speech, that I made her almost burst her belly with laughing.

DONADO.

Nay, I think so, and what speech was't?   55

BERGETTO.

What did I say, Poggio?

POGGIO.

Forsooth, my master said that he loved her almost as well
as he loved parmasent, and swore (I'll be sworn for him)
that she wanted but such a nose as his was to be as pretty a
young woman as any was in Parma.   60

DONADO.

O gross!

BERGETTO.

Nay, uncle, then she ask'd me whether my father had any
more children than myself: and I said, "No, 'twere better
he should have had his brains knock'd out first."

DONADO.

This is intolerable.   65

BERGETTO.

Then said she, "Will Signor Donado your uncle leave you
all his wealth?"

DONADO.

Ha! that was good, did she harp upon that string?

---

47. *may-game*] laughing-stock, comic butt.
53. *Uds sa' me*] God save me.
58. *parmasent*] parmesan cheese.

BERGETTO.

> Did she harp upon that string? Ay, that she did. I answered,
> "Leave me all his wealth? Why, woman, he hath no other   70
> wit; if he had, he should hear on't to his everlasting glory
> and confusion: I know," quoth I, "I am his white boy, and
> will not be gull'd"; and with that she fell into a great smile
> and went away. Nay, I did fit her.

DONADO.

> Ah, sirrah, then I see there is no changing of nature. Well,   75
> Bergetto, I fear thou wilt be a very ass still.

BERGETTO.

> I should be sorry for that, uncle.

DONADO.

> Come, come you home with me; since you are no better a
> speaker, I'll have you write to her after some courtly manner,
> and enclose some rich jewel in the letter.   80

BERGETTO.

> Ay marry, that will be excellent.

DONADO.

> Peace, innocent.
> Once in my time I'll set my wits to school,
> If all fail, 'tis but the fortune of a fool.

BERGETTO.

> Poggio, 'twill do, Poggio.   *Exeunt.*   85

[II.i]   *Enter* Giovanni *and* Annabella, *as from their chamber.*

GIOVANNI.

> Come, Annabella: no more sister now,
> But love, a name more gracious; do not blush,
> Beauty's sweet wonder, but be proud to know
> That yielding thou hast conquer'd, and inflam'd
> A heart whose tribute is thy brother's life.   5

ANNABELLA.

> And mine is his. O, how these stol'n contents

---

71. *glory*] apparently a malapropism by Bergetto.
72. *white boy*] favorite.
74. *fit*] give an appropriate answer.

Would print a modest crimson on my cheeks,
Had any but my heart's delight prevail'd!

GIOVANNI.

I marvel why the chaster of your sex
Should think this pretty toy call'd maidenhead   10
So strange a loss, when, being lost, 'tis nothing,
And you are still the same.

ANNABELLA.   'Tis well for you;
Now you can talk.

GIOVANNI.   Music as well consists
In th' ear, as in the playing.

ANNABELLA.   O, y'are wanton;
Tell on't, y'are best: do.

GIOVANNI.   Thou wilt chide me then.   15
Kiss me: so; thus hung Jove on Leda's neck,
And suck'd divine ambrosia from her lips.
I envy not the mightiest man alive,
But hold myself in being king of thee
More great than were I king of all the world.   20
But I shall lose you, sweetheart.

ANNABELLA.   But you shall not.

GIOVANNI.

You must be married, mistress.

ANNABELLA.   Yes? To whom?

GIOVANNI.

Someone must have you.

ANNABELLA.   You must.

GIOVANNI.   Nay, some other.

ANABELLA.

Now prithee do not speak so: without jesting,
You'll make me weep in earnest.

GIOVANNI.   What, you will not!   25
But tell me, sweet, canst thou be dar'd to swear
That thou wilt live to me, and to no other?

ANNABELLA.

By both our loves I dare, for didst thou know,
My Giovanni, how all suitors seem

---

16. *Leda*] the mistress of Jove, who approached her in the form of a swan.

To my eyes hateful, thou wouldst trust me then.   30

GIOVANNI.

Enough, I take thy word. Sweet, we must part:
Remember what thou vow'st, keep well my heart.

ANNABELLA.

Will you be gone?

GIOVANNI.

I must.

ANNABELLA.

When to return?   35

GIOVANNI.

Soon.

ANNABELLA.

Look you do.

GIOVANNI.

Farewell.   *Exit.*

ANNABELLA.

Go where thou wilt, in mind I'll keep thee here,
And where thou art, I know I shall be there.   40
Guardian!

Enter Putana.

PUTANA.

Child, how is't, child? Well, thank Heaven, ha?

ANNABELLA.

O guardian, what a paradise of joy
Have I pass'd over!

PUTANA.

Nay, what a paradise of joy have you pass'd under! Why,   45
now I commend thee, charge: fear nothing, sweetheart;
what though he be your brother? Your brother's a man,
I hope, and I say still, if a young wench feel the fit upon her,
let her take anybody, father or brother, all is one.

ANNABELLA.

I would not have it known for all the world.   50

PUTANA.

Nor I, indeed, for the speech of the people; else 'twere
nothing.

FLORIO (*within*).

Daughter Annabella!

−24−

ANNABELLA.

O me, my father! —Here, sir! —Reach my work.

FLORIO (*within*).

What are you doing?

ANNABELLA.   So: let him come now.   55

Enter Florio, Richardetto *like a doctor of physic, and* Philotis *with a lute in her hand.*

FLORIO.

So hard at work? That's well, you lose no time.
Look, I have brought you company: here's one,
A learned doctor lately come from Padua,
Much skill'd in physic, and for that I see
You have of late been sickly, I entreated   60
This reverend man to visit you some time.

ANNABELLA.

Y'are very welcome, sir.

RICHARDETTO.   I thank you, mistress.
Loud fame in large report hath spoke your praise
As well for virtue as perfection:
For which I have been bold to bring with me   65
A kinswoman of mine, a maid, for song
And music one perhaps will give content;
Please you to know her.

ANNABELLA.   They are parts I love,
And she for them most welcome.

PHILOTIS.   Thank you, lady.

FLORIO.

Sir, now you know my house, pray make not strange,   70
And if you find my daughter need your art,
I'll be your paymaster.

RICHARDETTO.   Sir, what I am

56–61.] *Weber; prose in Q.*   72–73. Sir . . . command.] *Weber; one line in Q.*

---

54. *work*] needlework.
58. *Padua*] famous for the medical school of its university.
64. *perfection*] accomplishments.
68. *parts*] abilities.
70. *make not strange*] do not stand on ceremony.

She shall command.

FLORIO.   You shall bind me to you.
Daughter, I must have conference with you
About some matters that concerns us both.   75
Good master doctor, please you but walk in,
We'll crave a little of your cousin's cunning.
I think my girl hath not quite forgot
To touch an instrument: she could have done't;
We'll hear them both.   80

RICHARDETTO. I'll wait upon you, sir.   *Exeunt.*

[II.ii]   *Enter* Soranzo *in his study reading a book.*

SORANZO.
"Love's measure is extreme, the comfort, pain,
The life unrest, and the reward disdain."
What's here? Look't o'er again: 'tis so, so writes
This smooth licentious poet in his rhymes.
But Sannazar, thou liest, for had thy bosom   5
Felt such oppression as is laid on mine,
Thou wouldst have kiss'd the rod that made thee smart.
To work then, happy muse, and contradict
What Sannazar hath in his envy writ.
"Love's measure is the mean, sweet his annoys,   10
His pleasure's life, and his reward all joys."
Had Annabella liv'd when Sannazar
Did in his brief encomium celebrate
Venice, that queen of cities, he had left
That verse which gain'd him such a sum of gold,   15
And for one only look from Annabel
Had writ of her and her diviner cheeks.
O how my thoughts are—

VASQUES (*within*).
Pray forbear; in rules of civility, let me give notice on't: I

[II.ii]
7. thee] *Dodsley;* the *Q*.

---

77. *cunning*] skill.
[II.ii]
5. *Sannazar*] Jacopo Sannazaro (?1456–1530), an Italian poet, author of
a famous epigram praising Venice, for which the city lavishly rewarded him.

shall be tax'd of my neglect of duty and service.   20

SORANZO.

What rude intrusion interrupts my peace?

Can I be nowhere private?

VASQUES (*within*).

Troth you wrong your modesty.

SORANZO.

What's the matter, Vasques, who is't?

Enter Hippolita *and* Vasques.

HIPPOLITA.

'Tis I: 25

Do you know me now? Look, perjur'd man, on her

Whom thou and thy distracted lust have wrong'd.

Thy sensual rage of blood hath made my youth

A scorn to men and angels, and shall I

Be now a foil to thy unsated change?   30

Thou know'st, false wanton, when my modest fame

Stood free from stain or scandal, all the charms

Of hell or sorcery could not prevail

Against the honor of my chaster bosom.

Thine eyes did plead in tears, thy tongue in oaths   35

Such and so many, that a heart of steel

Would have been wrought to pity, as was mine:

And shall the conquest of my lawful bed,

My husband's death urg'd on by his disgrace,

My loss of womanhood, be ill rewarded   40

With hatred and contempt? No, know Soranzo,

I have a spirit doth as much distaste

The slavery of fearing thee, as thou

Dost loathe the memory of what hath pass'd.

SORANZO.

Nay, dear Hippolita—

HIPPOLITA.   Call me not dear,   45

Nor think with supple words to smooth the grossness

Of my abuses; 'tis not your new mistress,

Your goodly madam-merchant, shall triumph

On my dejection: tell her thus from me,

---

20. *tax'd of*] rebuked for.

30. *foil*] setting, background (to make his new love more enjoyable).

My birth was nobler and by much more free.   50
SORANZO.
      You are too violent.
HIPPOLITA.   You are too double
      In your dissimulation. Seest thou this,
      This habit, these black mourning-weeds of care?
      'Tis thou art cause of this, and hast divorc'd
      My husband from his life and me from him,   55
      And made me widow in my widowhood.
SORANZO.
      Will you yet hear?
HIPPOLITA.   More of thy perjuries?
      Thy soul is drown'd too deeply in those sins;
      Thou need'st not add to th' number.
SORANZO.   Then I'll leave you;
      You are past all rules of sense.
HIPPOLITA.   And thou of grace.   60
VASQUES.
      Fie, mistress, you are not near the limits of reason: if my lord
      had a resolution as noble as virtue itself, you take the course
      to unedge it all. Sir, I beseech you, do not perplex her;
      griefs, alas, will have a vent. I dare undertake Madam
      Hippolita will now freely hear you.   65
SORANZO.
      Talk to a woman frantic! Are these the fruits of your love?
HIPPOLITA.
      They are the fruits of thy untruth, false man:
      Didst thou not swear, whilst yet my husband liv'd,
      That thou wouldst wish no happiness on earth
      More than to call me wife? Didst thou not vow,   70
      When he should die, to marry me? For which,
      The devil in my blood, and thy protests,
      Caus'd me to counsel him to undertake
      A voyage to Ligorn, for that we heard
      His brother there was dead, and left a daughter   75

57. thy] *Q corr.;* the *Q uncorr.*

---

63. *unedge*] blunt, weaken.
72. *protests*] protestations.
74. *Ligorn*] Leghorn (Italian *Livorno*).

-28-

Young and unfriended, who, with much ado,
I wish'd him to bring hither: he did so,
And went; and as thou know'st died on the way.
Unhappy man, to buy his death so dear
With my advice! Yet thou for whom I did it   80
Forget'st thy vows, and leav'st me to my shame.
SORANZO.
    Who could help this?
HIPPOLITA.   Who? Perjur'd man, thou couldst,
If thou hadst faith or love.
SORANZO.   You are deceiv'd.
The vows I made, if you remember well,
Were wicked and unlawful: 'twere more sin   85
To keep them than to break them; as for me,
I cannot mask my penitence. Think thou
How much thou hast digress'd from honest shame
In bringing of a gentleman to death
Who was thy husband, such a one as he,   90
So noble in his quality, condition,
Learning, behavior, entertainment, love,
As Parma could not show a braver man.
VASQUES.
    You do not well, this was not your promise.
SORANZO.
    I care not; let her know her monstrous life.   95
Ere I'll be servile to so black a sin,
I'll be accurs'd. Woman, come here no more:
Learn to repent and die, for by my honor
I hate thee and thy lust: you have been too foul.   [*Exit.*]
VASQUES [*aside*].
    This part has been scurvily play'd.   100
HIPPOLITA.
    How foolishly this beast contemns his fate,
And shuns the use of that which I more scorn
Than I once lov'd, his love; but let him go.

97. accurs'd] *this edn.;* a Curse *Q
uncorr.;* a Coarse *Q corr.*

---

100. *scurvily play'd*] badly acted (Vasques thinks that Soranzo should have soothed Hippolita).

My vengeance shall give comfort to this woe.

She offers to go away.

VASQUES.

Mistress, mistress, Madam Hippolita, pray, a word or two!   105

HIPPOLITA.

With me, sir?

VASQUES.

With you, if you please.

HIPPOLITA.

What is't?

VASQUES.

I know you are infinitely mov'd now, and you think you
have cause: some I confess you have, but sure not so much as   110
you imagine.

HIPPOLITA.

Indeed?

VASQUES.

O, you were miserably bitter, which you followed even to
the last syllable. Faith, you were somewhat too shrewd;
by my life you could not have took my lord in a worse   115
time, since I first knew him: tomorrow you shall find him
a new man.

HIPPOLITA.

Well, I shall wait his leisure.

VASQUES.

Fie, this is not a hearty patience, it comes sourly from you;
troth, let me persuade you for once.   120

HIPPOLITA [*aside*].

I have it, and it shall be so; thanks, opportunity! [*To him.*]
Persuade me to what?

VASQUES.

Visit him in some milder temper. O if you could but master
a little your female spleen, how might you win him!

HIPPOLITA.

He will never love me. Vasques, thou hast been a too   125

---

104. this] *this edn.;* his *Q.*   105.]   *Weber;*   Mistress . . . Hippo-
                                           lita,/ Pray . . . two! *Q.*

114. *shrewd*] sharp, outspoken.

trusty servant to such a master, and I believe thy reward
in the end will fall out like mine.

VASQUES.

So perhaps too.

HIPPOLITA.

Resolve thyself it will. Had I one so true, so truly honest,
so secret to my counsels, as thou hast been to him and his, 130
I should think it a slight acquittance, not only to make
him master of all I have, but even of myself.

VASQUES.

O you are a noble gentlewoman!

HIPPOLITA.

Wilt thou feed always upon hopes? Well, I know thou art
wise, and seest the reward of an old servant daily, what it is. 135

VASQUES.

Beggary and neglect.

HIPPOLITA.

True: but Vasques, wert thou mine, and wouldst be
private to me and my designs, I here protest myself and
all what I can else call mine should be at thy dispose.

VASQUES [aside].

Work you that way, old mole? Then I have the wind of 140
you. [To her.] I were not worthy of it by any desert that
could lie within my compass; if I could—

HIPPOLITA.

What then?

VASQUES.

I should then hope to live in these my old years with rest
and security. 145

HIPPOLITA.

Give me thy hand: now promise but thy silence,
And help to bring to pass a plot I have;
And here in sight of Heaven, that being done,
I make thee lord of me and mine estate.

VASQUES.

Come, you are merry; this is such a happiness that I can 150

150–151.] Weber; Come . . . merry;/
This . . . can/ Neither . . . believe. Q.

---

140. have the wind] see your intention.

neither think or believe.

HIPPOLITA.

Promise thy secrecy, and 'tis confirm'd.

VASQUES.

Then here I call our good genii for witnesses, whatsoever
your designs are, or against whomsoever, I will not only
be a special actor therein, but never disclose it till it be   155
effected.

HIPPOLITA.

I take thy word, and with that, thee for mine;
Come then, let's more confer of this anon.
On this delicious bane my thoughts shall banquet:
Revenge shall sweeten what my griefs have tasted.   160

Exeunt.

[II.iii]   *Enter* Richardetto *and* Philotis.

RICHARDETTO.

Thou seest, my lovely niece, these strange mishaps,
How all my fortunes turn to my disgrace,
Wherein I am but as a looker-on,
Whiles others act my shame and I am silent.

PHILOTIS.

But uncle, wherein can this borrowed shape   5
Give you content?

RICHARDETTO.   I'll tell thee, gentle niece.
Thy wanton aunt in her lascivious riots
Lives now secure, thinks I am surely dead
In my late journey to Ligorn for you,
As I have caus'd it to be rumor'd out;   10
Now would I see with what an impudence
She gives scope to her loose adultery,
And how the common voice allows hereof:
Thus far I have prevail'd.

153. for witnesses] *Dodsley;* foe-
witnesses *Q.*

---

159. *bane*] poison.
[II.iii]
  5. *shape*] disguise (the robe of a doctor).
  13. *how . . . hereof*] what ordinary people think about her.

PHILOTIS.   Alas, I fear
   You mean some strange revenge.
RICHARDETTO.   O, be not troubled;   15
   Your ignorance shall plead for you in all.
   But to our business: what, you learn'd for certain
   How Signor Florio means to give his daughter
   In marriage to Soranzo?
PHILOTIS.   Yes, for certain.
RICHARDETTO.
   But how find you young Annabella's love   20
   Inclin'd to him?
PHILOTIS.   For aught I could perceive,
   She neither fancies him or any else.
RICHARDETTO.
   There's mystery in that which time must show.
   She us'd you kindly?
PHILOTIS.   Yes.
RICHARDETTO.   And crav'd your company?
PHILOTIS.
   Often.
RICHARDETTO. 'Tis well: it goes as I could wish.   25
   I am the doctor now, and as for you,
   None knows you; if all fail not, we shall thrive.
   But who comes here?

Enter Grimaldi.

        I know him: 'tis Grimaldi,
   A Roman and a soldier, near allied
   Unto the duke of Montferrato, one   30
   Attending on the nuncio of the pope
   That now resides in Parma, by which means
   He hopes to get the love of Annabella.
GRIMALDI.
   Save you, sir.
RICHARDETTO.   And you, sir.
GRIMALDI.   I have heard
   Of your approv'd skill, which through the city   35

---

   16. *Your . . . all*] You know nothing of my plans and cannot be held
responsible for them.

Is freely talk'd of, and would crave your aid.

RICHARDETTO.
    For what, sir?

GRIMALDI.   Marry, sir, for this—
    But I would speak in private.

RICHARDETTO.   Leave us, cousin.

                                       Exit Philotis.

GRIMALDI.
    I love fair Annabella, and would know
    Whether in art there may not be receipts   40
    To move affection.

RICHARDETTO.   Sir, perhaps there may,
    But these will nothing profit you.

GRIMALDI.   Not me?

RICHARDETTO.
    Unless I be mistook, you are a man
    Greatly in favor with the cardinal.

GRIMALDI.
    What of that?

RICHARDETTO.   In duty to his grace,   45
    I will be bold to tell you, if you seek
    To marry Florio's daughter, you must first
    Remove a bar 'twixt you and her.

GRIMALDI.   Who's that?

RICHARDETTO.
    Soranzo is the man that hath her heart,
    And while he lives, be sure you cannot speed.   50

GRIMALDI.
    Soranzo! What, mine enemy! Is't he?

RICHARDETTO.
    Is he your enemy?

GRIMALDI.   The man I hate
    Worse than confusion—
    I'll kill him straight.

RICHARDETTO.   Nay then, take mine advice,
    Even for his grace's sake, the cardinal: 55
    I'll find a time when he and she do meet,

---

40. art] *Dyce;* arts *Q.*   54. kill] *Q corr.;* tell *Q uncorr.*

40. *receipts*] recipes (love-potions).

Of which I'll give you notice, and to be sure
He shall not 'scape you, I'll provide a poison
To dip your rapier's point in; if he had
As many heads as Hydra had, he dies.   60
GRIMALDI.
    But shall I trust thee, doctor?
RICHARDETTO.   As yourself;
    Doubt not in aught. [*Aside.*] Thus shall the fates decree:
    By me Soranzo falls, that ruin'd me.   *Exeunt.*

[II.iv]   *Enter* Donado, Bergetto, *and* Poggio.
DONADO.
    Well, sir, I must be content to be both your secretary and
your messenger myself. I cannot tell what this letter may
work, but as sure as I am alive, if thou come once to talk
with her, I fear thou wilt mar whatsoever I make.
BERGETTO.
    You make, uncle? Why, am not I big enough to carry mine   5
own letter, I pray?
DONADO.
    Ay, ay, carry a fool's head o' thy own! Why, thou dunce,
wouldst thou write a letter and carry it thyself?
BERGETTO.
    Yes, that I would, and read it to her with my own mouth;
for you must think, if she will not believe me myself when   10
she hears me speak, she will not believe another's hand-
writing. O, you think I am a blockhead, uncle! No, sir,
Poggio knows I have indited a letter myself, so I have.
POGGIO.
    Yes, truly, sir; I have it in my pocket.
DONADO.
    A sweet one, no doubt; pray let's see't.   15
BERGETTO.
    I cannot read my own hand very well, Poggio; read it,
Poggio.
DONADO.
    Begin.

63. ruin'd] *Q corr.;* min'd *Q uncorr.*   [II.iv]
                                     16–17.] *Gifford;* I . . . Poggio;/ Read
                                     . . . Poggio. *Q.*

POGGIO (*reads*).

"Most dainty and honey-sweet mistress, I could call you
fair, and lie as fast as any that loves you, but my uncle 20
being the elder man, I leave it to him, as more fit for his age
and the color of his beard. I am wise enough to tell you I
can bourd where I see occasion: or if you like my uncle's
wit better than mine, you shall marry me; if you like mine
better than his, I will marry you in spite of your teeth. So 25
commending my best parts to you, I rest—Yours upwards
and downwards, or you may choose, Bergetto."

BERGETTO.

Aha, here's stuff, uncle.

DONADO.

Here's stuff indeed to shame us all. Pray whose advice
did you take in this learned letter? 30

POGGIO.

None, upon my word, but mine own.

BERGETTO.

And mine, uncle, believe it, nobody's else; 'twas mine
own brain, I thank a good wit for't.

DONADO.

Get you home, sir, and look you keep within doors till I
return. 35

BERGETTO.

How! That were a jest indeed; I scorn it i'faith.

DONADO.

What! You do not?

BERGETTO.

Judge me, but I do now.

POGGIO.

Indeed, sir, 'tis very unhealthy.

DONADO.

Well, sir, if I hear any of your apish running to motions 40
and fopperies, till I come back, you were as good not; look
to't.   *Exit* Donado.

29–30.] *Weber;* Here's . . . all./ Pray 41. not] *Dodsley;* no *Q*.
. . . letter? *Q*.

---

23. *bourd*] jest.
40. *motions*] puppet-shows.

BERGETTO.

    Poggio, shall's steal to see this horse with the head in's tail?

POGGIO.

    Ay, but you must take heed of whipping.

BERGETTO.

    Dost take me for a child, Poggio? Come, honest Poggio.   45

                                        Exeunt.

[II.v]   *Enter* Friar *and* Giovanni.

FRIAR.

    Peace! Thou hast told a tale, whose every word

    Threatens eternal slaughter to the soul.

    I'm sorry I have heard it; would mine ears

    Had been one minute deaf, before the hour

    That thou cam'st to me. O young man castaway,   5

    By the religious number of mine order,

    I day and night have wak'd my aged eyes,

    Above my strength, to weep on thy behalf:

    But Heaven is angry, and be thou resolv'd,

    Thou art a man remark'd to taste a mischief: 10

    Look for't; though it come late, it will come sure.

GIOVANNI.

    Father, in this you are uncharitable;

    What I have done, I'll prove both fit and good.

    It is a principle, which you have taught

    When I was yet your scholar, that the frame   15

    And composition of the mind doth follow

    The frame and composition of the body:

    So where the body's furniture is beauty,

    The mind's must needs be virtue; which allowed,

    Virtue itself is reason but refin'd,   20

    And love the quintessence of that. This proves

45.] *Weber;* Dost . . . Poggio?/ Come   [II.v]
. . . Poggio. *Q.*   8. my] *Dodsley;* thy *Q.*
                                    15. frame] *Dodsley;* fame *Q.*
                                    17. the body] *Gifford;* body *Q.*

---

    6. *number*] Possibly meaning "group" or "company;" Gifford suggests an
emendation to "founder."

    10. *remark'd*] marked out.

    10. *mischief*] misfortune, distress.

    My sister's beauty being rarely fair
    Is rarely virtuous; chiefly in her love,
    And chiefly in that love, her love to me.
    If hers to me, then so is mine to her;   25
    Since in like causes are effects alike.

FRIAR.

    O ignorance in knowledge! Long ago,
    How often have I warn'd thee this before?
    Indeed, if we were sure there were no deity,
    Nor Heaven nor hell, then to be led alone   30
    By nature's light, as were philosophers
    Of elder times, might instance some defense.
    But 'tis not so; then, madman, thou wilt find
    That nature is in Heaven's positions blind.

GIOVANNI.

    Your age o'errules you; had you youth like mine,   35
    You'd make her love your Heaven, and her divine.

FRIAR.

    Nay then, I see thou'rt too far sold to hell,
    It lies not in the compass of my prayers
    To call thee back; yet let me counsel thee:
    Persuade thy sister to some marriage.   40

GIOVANNI.

    Marriage? Why, that's to damn her! That's to prove
    Her greedy of variety of lust.

FRIAR.

    O fearful! If thou wilt not, give me leave
    To shrive her, lest she should die unabsolv'd.

GIOVANNI.

    At your best leisure, father; then she'll tell you   45
    How dearly she doth prize my matchless love.
    Then you will know what pity 'twere we two
    Should have been sunder'd from each other's arms.
    View well her face, and in that little round
    You may observe a world of variety: 50
    For color, lips; for sweet perfumes, her breath;

---

   32. *elder times*] in the days of paganism, before Christianity had been revealed.

   34. *positions*] doctrines (implying that the study of nature will teach us nothing about God).

For jewels, eyes; for threads of purest gold,
Hair; for delicious choice of flowers, cheeks;
Wonder in every portion of that throne:
Hear her but speak, and you will swear the spheres   55
Make music to the citizens in Heaven.
But, father, what is else for pleasure fram'd,
Lest I offend your ears, shall go unnam'd.

FRIAR.

The more I hear, I pity thee the more,
That one so excellent should give those parts   60
All to a second death; what I can do
Is but to pray: and yet I could advise thee,
Wouldst thou be rul'd.

GIOVANNI.   In what?

FRIAR.   Why, leave her yet;
The throne of mercy is above your trespass,
Yet time is left you both—

GIOVANNI.   To embrace each other,   65
Else let all time be struck quite out of number.
She is like me, and I like her, resolv'd.

FRIAR.

No more! I'll visit her; this grieves me most,
Things being thus, a pair of souls are lost.   *Exeunt.*

[II.vi]   *Enter* Florio, Donado, Annabella, Putana.

FLORIO.

Where's Giovanni?

ANNABELLA.   Newly walk'd abroad,
And, as I heard him say, gone to the friar,
His reverend tutor.

FLORIO.   That's a blessed man,
A man made up of holiness; I hope
He'll teach him how to gain another world.   5

DONADO.

Fair gentlewoman, here's a letter sent
To you from my young cousin; I dare swear
He loves you in his soul: would you could hear

---

54. *throne*] Presumably Giovanni sees Annabella's face as the throne for
her mind or soul, though the text may be corrupt.
61. *second death*] damnation as well as physical death.

  Sometimes what I see daily, sighs and tears,
  As if his breast were prison to his heart.   10
FLORIO.
  Receive it, Annabella.
ANNABELLA.
  Alas, good man.
DONADO.
  What's that she said?
PUTANA.
  An't please you, sir, she said, "Alas, good man." Truly
  I do commend him to her every night before her first 15
  sleep, because I would have her dream of him, and she hear-
  kens to that most religiously.
DONADO.
  Say'st so? God a-mercy, Putana, there's something for thee
  [*gives her money*], and prithee do what thou canst on his
  behalf; sha' not be lost labor, take my word for't.   20
PUTANA.
  Thank you most heartily, sir; now I have a feeling of your
  mind, let me alone to work.
ANNABELLA.
  Guardian!
PUTANA.
  Did you call?
ANNABELLA.
  Keep this letter.   25
DONADO.
  Signor Florio, in any case bid her read it instantly.
FLORIO.
  Keep it for what? Pray read it me hereright.
ANNABELLA.
  I shall, sir.   *She reads.*
DONADO.
  How d'ee find her inclin'd, signor?
FLORIO.
  Troth, sir, I know not how; not all so well   30
  As I could wish.

14. An't] *Weber;* And *Q*.

___

 27. *hereright*] immediately.

ANNABELLA.

    Sir, I am bound to rest your cousin's debtor.

    The jewel I'll return; for if he love,

    I'll count that love a jewel.

DONADO.   Mark you that?

    Nay, keep them both, sweet maid.

ANNABELLA.   You must excuse me;   35

    Indeed I will not keep it.

FLORIO.   Where's the ring,

    That which your mother in her will bequeath'd,

    And charg'd you on her blessing not to give't

    To any but your husband? Send back that.

ANNABELLA.

    I have it not.

FLORIO.   Ha, have it not! Where is't?   40

ANNABELLA.

    My brother in the morning took it from me,

    Said he would wear't today.

FLORIO.   Well, what do you say

    To young Bergetto's love? Are you content

    To match with him? Speak.

DONADO.   There's the point indeed.

ANNABELLA [*aside*].

    What shall I do? I must say something now.   45

FLORIO.

    What say? Why d'ee not speak?

ANNABELLA.   Sir, with your leave,

    Please you to give me freedom?

FLORIO.   Yes, you have it.

ANNABELLA.

    Signor Donado, if your nephew mean

    To raise his better fortunes in his match,

    The hope of me will hinder such a hope;   50

    Sir, if you love him, as I know you do,

    Find one more worthy of his choice than me.

    In short, I'm sure I sha' not be his wife.

DONADO.

    Why, here's plain dealing, I commend thee for't,

47. have it] *Gifford;* have *Q.*

And all the worst I wish thee is, Heaven bless thee!   55
Your father yet and I will still be friends,
Shall we not, Signor Florio?

FLORIO.   Yes, why not?
Look, here your cousin comes.

Enter Bergetto *and* Poggio.

DONADO [*aside*].
O coxcomb, what doth he make here?

BERGETTO.
Where's my uncle, sirs?   60

DONADO.
What's the news now?

BERGETTO.
Save you, uncle, save you! You must not think I come
for nothing, masters: and how, and how is't? What, you
have read my letter? Ah, there I—tickled you i'faith!

POGGIO.
But 'twere better you had tickled her in another place.   65

BERGETTO.
Sirrah sweetheart, I'll tell thee a good jest; and riddle what
'tis.

ANNABELLA.
You say you'd tell me.

BERGETTO.
As I was walking just now in the street, I met a swaggering
fellow would needs take the wall of me, and because he   70
did thrust me, I very valiantly call'd him rogue. He here-
upon bade me draw: I told him I had more wit than so,
but when he saw that I would not, he did so maul me with
the hilts of his rapier that my head sung whilst my feet
caper'd in the kennel.   75

---

59. *make*] do.
70. *take the wall*] walk nearest to the wall, on the cleanest part of the
street.
75. *kennel*] gutter.

DONADO [aside].

Was ever the like ass seen?

ANNABELLA.

And what did you all this while?

BERGETTO.

Laugh at him for a gull, till I see the blood run about
mine ears, and then I could not choose but find in my
heart to cry; till a fellow with a broad beard—they say   80
he is a new-come doctor—call'd me into his house, and
gave me a plaster—look you, here 'tis—and, sir, there was
a young wench wash'd my face and hands most excellently,
i'faith, I shall love her as long as I live for't, did she not,
Poggio?   85

POGGIO.

Yes, and kiss'd him too.

BERGETTO.

Why, la now, you think I tell a lie, uncle, I warrant.

DONADO.

Would he that beat thy blood out of thy head had beaten
some wit into it; for I fear thou never wilt have any.

BERGETTO.

O, uncle, but there was a wench would have done a man's   90
heart good to have look'd on her—by this light she had
a face methinks worth twenty of you, Mistress Annabella.

DONADO.

Was ever such a fool born?

ANNABELLA.

I am glad she lik'd you, sir.

BERGETTO.

Are you so? By my troth I thank you, forsooth.   95

FLORIO.

Sure 'twas the doctor's niece, that was last day with us here.

BERGETTO.

'Twas she, 'twas she.

DONADO.

How do you know that, simplicity?

81. his] *Gifford;* this *Q.*

94. *lik'd*] pleased.

BERGETTO.

Why, does not he say so? If I should have said no, I should
have given him the lie, uncle, and so have deserv'd a dry 100
beating again; I'll none of that.

FLORIO.

A very modest well-behav'd young maid
As I have seen.

DONADO.   Is she indeed?

FLORIO.   Indeed

She is, if I have any judgment.

DONADO.

Well, sir, now you are free, you need not care for sending 105
letters: now you are dismiss'd, your mistress here will none
of you.

BERGETTO.

No? Why, what care I for that? I can have wenches
enough in Parma for half-a-crown apiece, cannot I, Poggio?

POGGIO.

I'll warrant you, sir.   110

DONADO.

Signor Florio,
I thank you for your free recourse you gave
For my admittance; and to you, fair maid,
That jewel I will give you 'gainst your marriage.
Come, will you go, sir?   115

BERGETTO.

Ay, marry will I. Mistress, farewell, mistress: I'll come
again tomorrow. Farewell, mistress.

Exit Donado, Bergetto, *and* Poggio.

Enter Giovanni.

FLORIO.

Son, where have you been? What, alone, alone still?
I would not have it so, you must forsake

102–103. A . . . seen.] *Weber; one line*   118–121.] *Weber; prose in Q.*
in Q.   118. still] *Gifford;* still, still *Q.*
111–115.] *Dyce; prose in Q.*

109. *half-a-crown*] the standard price of a prostitute.
114. *'gainst*] against, in anticipation of.

This over-bookish humor. Well, your sister   120
Hath shook the fool off.

GIOVANNI.   'Twas no match for her.

FLORIO.

'Twas not indeed, I meant it nothing less;
Soranzo is the man I only like—
Look on him, Annabella. Come, 'tis supper-time,
And it grows late.   *Exit* Florio.   125

GIOVANNI.

Whose jewel's that?

ANNABELLA.   Some sweetheart's.

GIOVANNI.   So I think.

ANNABELLA.

A lusty youth,
Signor Donado, gave it me to wear
Against my marriage.

GIOVANNI.   But you shall not wear it:
Send it him back again.

ANNABELLA.   What, you are jealous?   130

GIOVANNI.

That you shall know anon, at better leisure.
Welcome, sweet night! The evening crowns the day.

                                            Exeunt.

[III.i]   *Enter* Bergetto *and* Poggio.

BERGETTO.

Does my uncle think to make me a baby still? No, Poggio,
he shall know I have a sconce now.

POGGIO.

Ay, let him not bob you off like an ape with an apple.

BERGETTO.

'Sfoot, I will have the wench if he were ten uncles, in despite
of his nose, Poggio.   5

127–129. A . . . marriage. *Gifford;*   129–130. But . . . again.] *Gifford; one*
A . . . me/ To . . . marriage. *Q*.   *line in Q*.

2. *sconce*] head, brain.
3. *bob*] fob, trick.

POGGIO.

> Hold him to the grindstone and give not a jot of ground.
> She hath in a manner promised you already.

BERGETTO.

> True, Poggio, and her uncle the doctor swore I should
> marry her.

POGGIO.

> He swore, I remember.   10

BERGETTO.

> And I will have her, that's more; didst see the codpiece-
> point she gave me and the box of marmalade?

POGGIO.

> Very well; and kiss'd you, that my chops water'd at the
> sight on't. There's no way but to clap up a marriage in
> hugger-mugger.   15

BERGETTO.

> I will do't; for I tell thee, Poggio, I begin to grow valiant
> methinks, and my courage begins to rise.

POGGIO.

> Should you be afraid of your uncle?

BERGETTO.

> Hang him, old doting rascal! No, I say I will have her.

POGGIO.

> Lose no time then.   20

BERGETTO.

> I will beget a race of wise men and constables, that shall
> cart whores at their own charges, and break the duke's
> peace ere I have done myself. —Come away.   *Exeunt.*

6–7.] *Weber;* Hold . . . ground./ She   8–9.] *Weber;* True . . . doctor/ Swore
. . . already. *Q.*   . . . her. *Q.*
8. S. P. BERGETTO] *Dodsley; Poggio Q.*

11–12. *codpiece-point*] a lace for tying the codpiece, defined by *OED* as
"a bagged appendage to the front of the close-fitting hose or breeches worn
by men from the 15th to the 17th c.; often conspicuous and ornamented."
    14–15. *in hugger-mugger*] secretly.
    22. *cart whores*] Part of the traditional punishment for prostitutes was to
parade them through the streets in a cart or wagon.

[III.ii]

Enter Florio, Giovanni, Soranzo, Annabella, Putana, *and* Vasques.

FLORIO.

    My Lord Soranzo, though I must confess
    The proffers that are made me have been great
    In marriage of my daughter, yet the, hope
    Of your still rising honors have prevail'd
    Above all other jointures; here she is: 5
    She knows my mind, speak for yourself to her,
    And hear you, daughter, see you use him nobly;
    For any private speech I'll give you time.
    Come, son, and you the rest, let them alone:
    Agree they as they may.

SORANZO.   I thank you, sir.   10

GIOVANNI [*aside to* Annabella].

    Sister, be not all woman, think on me.

SORANZO.

    Vasques.

VASQUES.

    My Lord?

SORANZO.

    Attend me without.

                   Exeunt omnes, manet Soranzo *and* Annabella.

ANNABELLA.

    Sir, what's your will with me?

SORANZO.   Do you not know   15
    What I should tell you?

ANNABELLA.   Yes, you'll say you love me.

SORANZO.

    And I'll swear it too; will you believe it?

ANNABELLA.

    'Tis no point of faith.

               Enter Giovanni *above.*

SORANZO.   Have you not will to love?

10. Agree they] *Gifford;* Agree *Q.*   18. no] *Gifford;* not *Q.*
15–16. Do . . . you?] *Weber; one line*
in Q.

---

5. *jointures*] Apparently a reference to Donado's offer at I.iii.14–18.
14.1 *manet*] remain.

−47−

ANNABELLA.

    Not you.

SORANZO.   Whom then?

ANNABELLA.   That's as the fates infer.

GIOVANNI [*aside*].

    Of those I'm regent now.

SORANZO.   What mean you, sweet?   20

ANNABELLA.

    To live and die a maid.

SORANZO.   O, that's unfit.

GIOVANNI [*aside*].

    Here's one can say that's but a woman's note.

SORANZO.

    Did you but see my heart, then would you swear—

ANNABELLA.

    That you were dead.

GIOVANNI [*aside*].   That's true, or somewhat near it.

SORANZO.

    See you these true love's tears?

ANNABELLA.   No.

GIOVANNI [*aside*].   Now she winks.   25

SORANZO.

    They plead to you for grace.

ANNABELLA.   Yet nothing speak.

SORANZO.

    O grant my suit!

ANNABELLA.   What is't?

SORANZO.   To let me live—

ANNABELLA.

    Take it.

SORANZO.   —Still yours.

ANNABELLA.   That is not mine to give.

GIOVANNI [*aside*].

    One such another word would kill his hopes.

SORANZO.

    Mistress, to leave those fruitless strifes of wit,   30

    Know I have lov'd you long and lov'd you truly:

---

31. Know] *Dodsley;* I know *Q.*

Not hope of what you have, but what you are,
Have drawn me on; then let me not in vain
Still feel the rigor of your chaste disdain.
I'm sick, and sick to th' heart.

ANNABELLA.   Help, aqua-vitae!   35

SORANZO.
  What mean you?

ANNABELLA.   Why, I thought you had been sick.

SORANZO.
  Do you mock my love?

GIOVANNI [aside].   There, sir, she was too nimble.

SORANZO [aside].
  'Tis plain, she laughs at me. [To her.] These scornful taunts
  Neither become your modesty or years.

ANNABELLA.
  You are no looking glass; or if you were,   40
  I'd dress my language by you.

GIOVANNI [aside].   I'm confirm'd.

ANNABELLA.
  To put you out of doubt, my lord, methinks
  Your common sense should make you understand
  That if I lov'd you, or desir'd your love,
  Some way I should have given you better taste: 45
  But since you are a nobleman, and one
  I would not wish should spend his youth in hopes,
  Let me advise you to forbear your suit,
  And think I wish you well, I tell you this.

SORANZO.
  Is't you speak this?

ANNABELLA.   Yes, I myself; yet know—   50
  Thus far I give you comfort—if mine eyes
  Could have pick'd out a man amongst all those
  That sued to me, to make a husband of,
  You should have been that man. Let this suffice;
  Be noble in your secrecy and wise.   55

GIOVANNI [aside].
  Why, now I see she loves me.

38–49.] Dodsley; prose in Q.   48. to] Gifford; here, to Q.

35. aqua-vitae] brandy, here to be used medicinally.

ANNABELLA.   One word more:
As ever virtue liv'd within your mind,
As ever noble courses were your guide,
As ever you would have me know you lov'd me,
Let not my father know hereof by you;   60
If I hereafter find that I must marry,
It shall be you or none.

SORANZO.   I take that promise.

ANNABELLA.
O, O, my head!

SORANZO.
What's the matter? Not well?

ANNABELLA.
O, I begin to sicken.   65

GIOVANNI [aside].
Heaven forbid!   *Exit from above.*

SORANZO.
Help, help within there, ho!

Enter Florio, Giovanni, Putana.

Look to your daughter, Signor Florio.

FLORIO.
Hold her up, she swoons.

GIOVANNI.
Sister, how d'ee?   70

ANNABELLA.
Sick—brother, are you there?

FLORIO.
Convey her to her bed instantly, whilst I send for a physician;
quickly, I say.

PUTANA.
Alas, poor child!   *Exeunt, manet* Soranzo.

Enter Vasques.

VASQUES.
My lord?   75

SORANZO.
O Vasques, now I doubly am undone
Both in my present and my future hopes;

67.1.] *Weber; after l. 68 in Q.*   68.] *Assigned to Soranzo by Gifford; to
Giovanni in Q.*

She plainly told me that she could not love,
And thereupon soon sicken'd, and I fear
Her life's in danger.   80

VASQUES [*aside*].

By'r lady, sir, and so is yours, if you knew all. [*To him.*]
'Las, sir, I am sorry for that; may be 'tis but the maid's-
sickness, an over-flux of youth, and then, sir, there is no such
present remedy as present marriage. But hath she given you
an absolute denial?   85

SORANZO.

She hath and she hath not; I'm full of grief,
But what she said I'll tell thee as we go.   *Exeunt.*

[III.iii]   *Enter* Giovanni *and* Putana.

PUTANA.

O sir, we are all undone, quite undone, utterly undone,
and sham'd forever; your sister, O your sister!

GIOVANNI.

What of her? For Heaven's sake, speak, how does she?

PUTANA.

O that ever I was born to see this day!

GIOVANNI.

She is not dead, ha? Is she?   5

PUTANA.

Dead? No, she is quick; 'tis worse, she is with child. You
know what you have done; Heaven forgive 'ee! 'Tis too late
to repent now, Heaven help us.

GIOVANNI.

With child? How dost thou know't?

PUTANA.

How do I know't? Am I at these years ignorant what the   10

6–8.] *Weber;* Dead . . . child./ You
. . . 'ee!/ 'Tis . . . us. *Q.*

82–83. *maid's-sickness*] otherwise called green-sickness, a form of anemia
affecting young girls.
    84. *present*] immediate.
[III.iii]
    6. *quick*] a play on two meanings of the word: (1) alive; (2) pregnant.

meanings of qualms and water-pangs be? Of changing of
colors, queasiness of stomachs, pukings, and another
thing that I could name? Do not, for her and your credit's
sake, spend the time in asking how, and which way, 'tis so;
she is quick, upon my word: if you let a physician see her   15
water, y'are undone.

GIOVANNI.

But in what case is she?

PUTANA.

Prettily amended; 'twas but a fit which I soon espied,
and she must look for often henceforward.

GIOVANNI.

Commend me to her, bid her take no care;   20
Let not the doctor visit her, I charge you,
Make some excuse, till I return. —O me!
I have a world of business in my head.
Do not discomfort her.—
How does this news perplex me! —If my father   25
Come to her, tell him she's recover'd well,
Say 'twas but some ill diet; d'ee hear, woman?
Look you to't.

PUTANA.

I will, sir.   *Exeunt.*

[III.iv]   *Enter* Florio *and* Richardetto.

FLORIO.

And how d'ee find her, sir?

RICHARDETTO.   Indifferent well;
I see no danger, scarce perceive she's sick,
But that she told me, she had lately eaten
Melons, and, as she thought, those disagreed
With her young stomach.

FLORIO.   Did you give her aught?   5

24–26.] *Gifford;* Do . . . me!/ If . . .   25. does] *Dodsley;* doe *Q.*
well, *Q.*

---

17. *case*] condition.
20. *take no care*] not worry.

RICHARDETTO.
>An easy surfeit-water, nothing else.
>You need not doubt her health; I rather think
>Her sickness is a fulness of her blood—
>You understand me?

FLORIO.   I do; you counsel well,
>And once, within these few days, will so order't   10
>She shall be married ere she know the time.

RICHARDETTO.
>Yet let not haste, sir, make unworthy choice;
>That were dishonor.

FLORIO.   Master Doctor, no;
>I will not do so neither; in plain words,
>My Lord Soranzo is the man I mean.   15

RICHARDETTO.
>A noble and a virtuous gentleman.

FLORIO.
>As any is in Parma. Not far hence
>Dwells Father Bonaventure, a grave friar,
>Once tutor to my son; now at his cell
>I'll have 'em married.

RICHARDETTO.   You have plotted wisely.   20

FLORIO.
>I'll send one straight to speak with him tonight.

RICHARDETTO.
>Soranzo's wise, he will delay no time.

FLORIO.
>It shall be so.

>>>*Enter* Friar *and* Giovanni.

FRIAR.   Good peace be here and love.

FLORIO.
>Welcome, religious friar; you are one
>That still bring blessing to the place you come to.   25

GIOVANNI.
>Sir, with what speed I could, I did my best

21.] *Weber;* I'll . . . straight/ To . . .
tonight.*Q*.

---

6. *easy surfeit-water*] mild cure for indigestion.

> To draw this holy man from forth his cell
> To visit my sick sister, that with words
> Of ghostly comfort, in this time of need,
> He might absolve her, whether she live or die.   30

FLORIO.

> 'Twas well done, Giovanni; thou herein
> Hast showed a Christian's care, a brother's love.
> Come, father, I'll conduct you to her chamber,
> And one thing would entreat you.

FRIAR.   Say on, sir.

FLORIO.

> I have a father's dear impression,   35
> And wish, before I fall into my grave,
> That I might see her married, as 'tis fit;
> A word from you, grave man, will win her more
> Than all our best persuasions.

FRIAR.   Gentle sir,

> All this I'll say, that Heaven may prosper her.   *Exeunt.*   40

[III.v]   *Enter* Grimaldi.

GRIMALDI.

> Now if the doctor keep his word, Soranzo,
> Twenty to one you miss your bride; I know
> 'Tis an unnoble act, and not becomes
> A soldier's valor, but in terms of love,
> Where merit cannot sway, policy must.   5
> I am resolv'd; if this physician
> Play not on both hands, then Soranzo falls.

Enter Richardetto.

RICHARDETTO.

> You are come as I could wish; this very night

8–11. You . . . Married.] *Dodsley;*
prose in Q.

---

29. *ghostly*] spiritual.

35. *impression*] The meaning is not clear. Perhaps it might be paraphrased as "notion" or "idea" (of the sort that fathers usually have).
[III.v]

5. *policy*] cunning.

7. *Play . . . hands*] is not acting as a double-agent, working for both sides.

Soranzo, 'tis ordain'd, must be affied
To Annabella, and, for aught I know,   10
Married.

GRIMALDI.   How!

RICHARDETTO.   Yet your patience.
The place, 'tis Friar Bonaventure's cell.
Now I would wish you to bestow this night
In watching thereabouts; 'tis but a night:
If you miss now, tomorrow I'll know all.   15

GRIMALDI.
Have you the poison?

RICHARDETTO.   Here 'tis in this box.
Doubt nothing, this will do't; in any case,
As you respect your life, be quick and sure.

GRIMALDI.
I'll speed him.

RICHARDETTO.   Do; away! for 'tis not safe
You should be seen much here. —Ever my love!   20

GRIMALDI.
And mine to you.   *Exit* Grimaldi.

RICHARDETTO.
So; if this hit, I'll laugh and hug revenge,
And they that now dream of a wedding-feast
May chance to mourn the lusty bridegroom's ruin.
But to my other business. —Niece Philotis!   25

Enter Philotis.

PHILOTIS.
Uncle?

RICHARDETTO.
My lovely niece!
You have bethought 'ee?

PHILOTIS.   Yes, and, as you counsel'd,
Fashion'd my heart to love him; but he swears
He will tonight be married, for he fears   30
His uncle else, if he should know the drift,

27–28. My . . . bethought 'ee?] *Gifford; one line in Q.*

---

9. *affied*] affianced, betrothed.

Will hinder all, and call his coz to shrift.

RICHARDETTO.
Tonight? Why, best of all!—but let me see,
I—ha—yes: so it shall be; in disguise
We'll early to the friar's, I have thought on't.   35

Enter Bergetto *and* Poggio.

PHILOTIS.
Uncle, he comes.
RICHARDETTO.   Welcome, my worthy coz.
BERGETTO.
Lass, pretty lass, come buss, lass! —Aha, Poggio!
                                               [*Kisses her.*]

POGGIO.
There's hope of this yet!
RICHARDETTO.
You shall have time enough; withdraw a little,
We must confer at large.   40
BERGETTO.
Have you not sweetmeats or dainty devices for me?
PHILOTIS.
You shall have enough, sweetheart.
BERGETTO.
Sweetheart! Mark that, Poggio! By my troth, I cannot choose
but kiss thee once more for that word "sweetheart."—
Poggio, I have a monstrous swelling about my stomach,   45
whatsoever the matter be.
POGGIO.
You shall have physic for't, sir.
RICHARDETTO.
Time runs apace.
BERGETTO.
Time's a blockhead.
RICHARDETTO.
Be rul'd; when we have done what's fit to do,   50
Then you may kiss your fill, and bed her too.   *Exeunt.*

38. S. P. POGGIO] *this edn.; Philotis, Q.*   42. shall have] *Gifford;* shall *Q.*
Richardetto, Gifford.

_____

37. *buss*] kiss.

[III.vi]

Enter the Friar *sitting in a chair,* Annabella *kneeling and whispering to him: a table before them and wax-lights: she weeps and wrings her hands.*

FRIAR.

    I am glad to see this penance; for, believe me,
    You have unripp'd a soul so foul and guilty
    As I must tell you true, I marvel how
    The earth hath borne you up: but weep, weep on,
    These tears may do you good; weep faster yet,   5
    Whiles I do read a lecture.

ANNABELLA.   Wretched creature!

FRIAR.

    Ay, you are wretched, miserably wretched,
    Almost condemn'd alive. There is a place—
    List, daughter—in a black and hollow vault,
    Where day is never seen; there shines no sun,   10
    But flaming horror of consuming fires,
    A lightless sulphur, chok'd with smoky fogs
    Of an infected darkness; in this place
    Dwell many thousand thousand sundry sorts
    Of never-dying deaths; there damned souls   15
    Roar without pity; there are gluttons fed
    With toads and adders; there is burning oil
    Pour'd down the drunkard's throat; the usurer
    Is forc'd to sup whole draughts of molten gold;
    There is the murderer forever stabb'd,   20
    Yet can he never die; there lies the wanton
    On racks of burning steel, whiles in his soul
    He feels the torment of his raging lust.

ANNABELLA.

    Mercy, O mercy!

FRIAR.   There stands these wretched things
    Who have dream'd out whole years in lawless sheets   25
    And secret incests, cursing one another:

0.1. Friar] *Weber;* Friar *in his study Q*.

    0.1.] *Q's in his study* clearly seems an error, as the scene takes place in Annabella's bedroom (see III.iv.33).
    6. *read a lecture*] deliver a rebuke.

    Then you will wish each kiss your brother gave
    Had been a dagger's point; then you shall hear
    How he will cry, "O would my wicked sister
    Had first been damn'd, when she did yield to lust!"—   30
    But soft, methinks I see repentance work
    New motions in your heart; say, how is't with you?

ANNABELLA.

    Is there no way left to redeem my miseries?

FRIAR.

    There is, despair not; Heaven is merciful,
    And offers grace even now. 'Tis thus agreed,   35
    First, for your honor's safety, that you marry
    The Lord Soranzo; next, to save your soul,
    Leave off this life, and henceforth live to him.

ANNABELLA.

    Ay me!

FRIAR.   Sigh not; I know the baits of sin
    Are hard to leave—O, 'tis a death to do't.   40
    Remember what must come. Are you content?

ANNABELLA.

    I am.

FRIAR.   I like it well; we'll take the time.
    Who's near us there?

               Enter Florio *and* Giovanni.

FLORIO.

    Did you call, father?

FRIAR.

    Is Lord Soranzo come?

FLORIO.   He stays below.   45

FRIAR.

    Have you acquainted him at full?

FLORIO.   I have,
    And he is overjoy'd.

FRIAR.   And so are we;
    Bid him come near.

46–47. I . . . overjoy'd.] *Weber; one*   47–48. And . . . near.] *Weber; one*
line in Q.   *line in* Q.

---

    42. *take the time*] seize the opportunity.

GIOVANNI [*aside*].   My sister weeping, ha?
    I fear this friar's falsehood. [*To him.*] I will call him.   *Exit.*
FLORIO.
    Daughter, are you resolv'd?
ANNABELLA.   Father, I am.   50
        Enter Giovanni, Soranzo, *and* Vasques.
FLORIO.
    My Lord Soranzo, here
    Give me your hand; for that I give you this.
                                [*Joins their hands.*]
SORANZO.
    Lady, say you so too?
ANNABELLA.   I do, and vow
    To live with you and yours.
FRIAR.   Timely resolv'd:
    My blessing rest on both; more to be done,   55
    You may perform it on the morning sun.   *Exeunt.*

[III.vii]   *Enter* Grimaldi *with his rapier drawn and a dark lantern.*

GRIMALDI.
    'Tis early night as yet, and yet too soon
    To finish such a work; here I will lie
    To listen who comes next.   *He lies down.*

Enter Bergetto *and* Philotis *disguis'd, and after* Richardetto *and* Poggio.

BERGETTO.
    We are almost at the place, I hope, sweetheart.
GRIMALDI [*aside*].
    I hear them near, and heard one say "sweetheart".   5
    'Tis he; now guide my hand, some angry justice,
    Home to his bosom. [*Aloud.*] Now have at you, sir!
                        Strikes Bergetto *and exit.*
BERGETTO.
    O help, help! Here's a stitch fallen in my guts, O for a
    flesh-tailor quickly!—Poggio!

48–49. My . . . him.] *Weber;* My . . .   53–54. I . . . yours.] *Weber; one line*
falsehood./ I . . . him. *Q.*   *in Q.*

---

9. *flesh-tailor*] surgeon.

PHILOTIS.

What ails my love? 10

BERGETTO.

I am sure I cannot piss forward and backward, and yet I
am wet before and behind. —Lights, lights! ho, lights!

PHILOTIS.

Alas, some villain here has slain my love!

RICHARDETTO.

O Heaven forbid it! —Raise up the next neighbors
Instantly, Poggio, and bring lights.   *Exit* Poggio. 15
How is't, Bergetto? Slain! It cannot be;
Are you sure y'are hurt?

BERGETTO.

O my belly seethes like a porridge-pot, some cold water,
I shall boil over else; my whole body is in a sweat, that you
may wring my shirt; feel here—Why, Poggio! 20

Enter Poggio *with* Officers *and lights and halberts.*

POGGIO.

Here! Alas, how do you?

RICHARDETTO.

Give me a light. What's here? All blood! O sirs,
Signor Donado's nephew now is slain.
Follow the murderer with all the haste
Up to the city, he cannot be far hence; 25
Follow, I beseech you.

OFFICERS.

Follow, follow, follow!   *Exeunt* Officers.

RICHARDETTO.

Tear off thy linen, coz, to stop his wounds;
Be of good comfort, man.

BERGETTO.

Is all this mine own blood? Nay, then, good night with 30
me. Poggio, commend me to my uncle, dost hear? Bid him
for my sake make much of this wench. O!—I am going

16–17.] *Gifford;* How . . . Slain!/ It
. . . hurt? *Q.*

---

32. *make much of*] take care of, treat generously.

the wrong way sure, my belly aches so. —O, farewell,
Poggio!—O!—O!—   *Dies.*

PHILOTIS.

   O, he is dead!

POGGIO.   How ! Dead!

RICHARDETTO.   He's dead indeed.   35
   'Tis now too late to weep; let's have him home,
   And with what speed we may, find out the murderer.

POGGIO.

   O my master, my master, my master!   *Exeunt.*

[III.viii]   *Enter* Vasques *and* Hippolita.

HIPPOLITA.

   Betroth'd?

VASQUES.

   I saw it.

HIPPOLITA.

   And when's the marriage-day?

VASQUES.

   Some two days hence.

HIPPOLITA.

   Two days! Why, man, I would but wish two hours   5
   To send him to his last and lasting sleep;
   And, Vasques, thou shalt see I'll do it bravely.

VASQUES.

   I do not doubt your wisdom, nor, I trust, you my secrecy;
   I am infinitely yours.

HIPPOLITA.

   I will be thine in spite of my disgrace.   10
   So soon? O, wicked man, I durst be sworn,
   He'd laugh to see me weep.

VASQUES.

   And that's a villainous fault in him.

HIPPOLITA.

   No, let him laugh, I'm arm'd in my resolves;
   Be thou still true.   15

VASQUES.

   I should get little by treachery against so hopeful a preferment as I am like to climb to.

HIPPOLITA.

> Even to my bosom, Vasques. Let my youth
> Revel in these new pleasures; if we thrive,
> He now hath but a pair of days to live.   *Exeunt.*   20

[III.ix]

> *Enter* Florio, Donado, Richardetto, Poggio, *and* Officers.

FLORIO.

> 'Tis bootless now to show yourself a child,
> Signor Donado; what is done, is done.
> Spend not the time in tears, but seek for justice.

RICHARDETTO.

> I must confess, somewhat I was in fault
> That had not first acquainted you what love   5
> Pass'd 'twixt him and my niece; but, as I live,
> His fortune grieves me as it were mine own.

DONADO.

> Alas, poor creature, he meant no man harm,
> That I am sure of.

FLORIO.   I believe that too.

> But stay, my masters, are you sure you saw   10
> The murderer pass here?

OFFICER.

> And it please you, sir, we are sure we saw a ruffian, with a
> naked weapon in his hand all bloody, get into my lord
> cardinal's grace's gate, that we are sure of; but for fear of
> his grace, bless us, we durst go no further.   15

DONADO.

> Know you what manner of man he was?

OFFICER.

> Yes, sure, I know the man, they say 'a is a soldier; he that
> lov'd your daughter, sir, an't please ye; 'twas he for certain.

FLORIO.

> Grimaldi, on my life!

OFFICER.   Ay, ay, the same.

---

18. *my youth*] a contemptuous reference to Soranzo.
[III.ix]
    17. *'a*] he.

RICHARDETTO.
>   The cardinal is noble; he no doubt   20
>   Will give true justice.

DONADO.
>   Knock someone at the gate.

POGGIO.
>   I'll knock, sir.   Poggio *knocks.*

SERVANT (*within*).
>   What would 'ee?

FLORIO.
>   We require speech with the lord cardinal   25
>   About some present business; pray inform
>   His grace that we are here.

Enter Cardinal *and* Grimaldi.

CARDINAL.
>   Why, how now, friends! What saucy mates are you,
>   That know nor duty nor civility?
>   Are we a person fit to be your host,   30
>   Or is our house become your common inn,
>   To beat our doors at pleasure? What such haste
>   Is yours as that it cannot wait fit times?
>   Are you the masters of this commonwealth,
>   And know no more discretion? O, your news   35
>   Is here before you; you have lost a nephew,
>   Donado, last night by Grimaldi slain:
>   Is that your business? Well, sir, we have knowledge on't.
>   Let that suffice.

GRIMALDI.   In presence of your grace,
>   In thought I never meant Bergetto harm.   40
>   But Florio, you can tell, with how much scorn
>   Soranzo, back'd with his confederates,
>   Hath often wrong'd me; I to be reveng'd,
>   (For that I could not win him else to fight)
>   Had thought by way of ambush to have kill'd him,   45
>   But was unluckily therein mistook,
>   Else he had felt what late Bergetto did:
>   And though my fault to him were merely chance,
>   Yet humbly I submit me to your grace,
>   To do with me as you please.   [*Kneels.*]

-63-

CARDINAL.   Rise up, Grimaldi.   50
    You citizens of Parma, if you seek
    For justice, know, as nuncio from the pope,
    For this offense I here receive Grimaldi
    Into his holiness' protection.
    He is no common man, but nobly born;   55
    Of princes' blood, though you, Sir Florio,
    Thought him too mean a husband for your daughter.
    If more you seek for, you must go to Rome,
    For he shall thither; learn more wit, for shame.
    Bury your dead. —Away, Grimaldi—leave 'em!   60
                      Exeunt Cardinal *and* Grimaldi.

DONADO.
    Is this a churchman's voice? Dwells justice here?

FLORIO.
    Justice is fled to Heaven and comes no nearer.
    Soranzo! Was't for him? O impudence!
    Had he the face to speak it, and not blush?
    Come, come, Donado, there's no help in this,   65
    When cardinals think murder's not amiss.
    Great men may do their wills, we must obey;
    But Heaven will judge them for't another day.   *Exeunt.*

[IV.i]
A Banquet. Hautboys. Enter the Friar, Giovanni, Annabella, Philotis,
Soranzo, Donado, Florio, Richardetto, Putana, *and* Vasques.

FRIAR.
    These holy rites perform'd, now take your times
    To spend the remnant of the day in feast;
    Such fit repasts are pleasing to the saints,
    Who are your guests, though not with mortal eyes
    To be beheld. —Long prosper in this day,   5
    You happy couple, to each other's joy!

---

    62. *fled to Heaven*] an allusion to the legend of Astraea, goddess of justice,
who fled to Heaven when the Golden Age of earth came to an end.
[IV.i]
    0.1. *A Banquet*] a dessert of confectionery, fruit, wine, etc.
    0.1. *Hautboy*] "A wooden double-reed wind instrument of high pitch"
(*OED*).

SORANZO.

    Father, your prayer is heard; the hand of goodness
    Hath been a shield for me against my death,
    And, more to bless me, hath enrich'd my life
    With this most precious jewel; such a prize   10
    As earth hath not another like to this.
    Cheer up, my love, and gentlemen, my friends,
    Rejoice with me in mirth; this day we'll crown
    With lusty cups to Annabella's health.

GIOVANNI (aside).

    O torture! Were the marriage yet undone,   15
    Ere I'd endure this sight, to see my love
    Clipp'd by another, I would dare confusion,
    And stand the horror of ten thousand deaths.

VASQUES.

    Are you not well, sir?

GIOVANNI.   Prithee, fellow, wait;

    I need not thy officious diligence.   20

FLORIO.

    Signor Donado, come, you must forget
    Your late mishaps, and drown your cares in wine.

SORANZO.

    Vasques!

VASQUES.   My lord?

SORANZO.   Reach me that weighty bowl.

    Here, brother Giovanni, here's to you;
    Your turn comes next, though now a bachelor.   25
    Here's to your sister's happiness and mine!

GIOVANNI.

    I cannot drink.

SORANZO.   What!

GIOVANNI.   'Twill indeed offend me.

ANNABELLA.

    Pray do not urge him, if he be not willing.   *Hautboys.*

28. S.D. *Hautboys*] Gifford; *after l. 35*
in Q.

---

17. *Clipp'd*] embraced.
19. *wait*] wait on the guests.

FLORIO.

How now, what noise is this?

VASQUES.

O, sir, I had forgot to tell you; certain young maidens   30
of Parma, in honor to Madam Annabella's marriage, have
sent their loves to her in a masque, for which they humbly
crave your patience and silence.

SORANZO.

We are much bound to them, so much the more
As it comes unexpected; guide them in.   35

Enter Hippolita *and Ladies in* [*masks and*] *white robes, with garlands of
willows. Music and a dance.*

Thanks, lovely virgins; now might we but know
To whom we have been beholding for this love,
We shall acknowledge it.

HIPPOLITA.   Yes, you shall know;   [*Unmasks.*]
What think you now?

OMNES.   Hippolita!

HIPPOLITA.   'Tis she,
Be not amaz'd; nor blush, young lovely bride,   40
I come not to defraud you of your man.
'Tis now no time to reckon up the talk
What Parma long hath rumor'd of us both:
Let rash report run on; the breath that vents it
Will, like a bubble, break itself at last.   45
But now to you, sweet creature: lend's your hand;
Perhaps it hath been said that I would claim
Some interest in Soranzo, now your lord.
What I have right to do, his soul knows best:
But in my duty to your noble worth,   50

34–35.] *Gifford; prose in Q*.   37. this] *Q corr.; thy Q uncorr.*
35.2. *a dance.*] *Weber; a dance.*
Dance. Q.

---

29. *noise*] music.
34. *bound*] obliged.
35.2. *willows*] An emblem of disappointed love. Cf. the willow song in
Othello, IV.iii.
37. *beholding*] indebted.

Sweet Annabella, and my care of you,
Here take, Soranzo, take this hand from me:
I'll once more join what by the holy church
Is finish'd and allow'd; have I done well?

SORANZO.
  You have too much engag'd us.
HIPPOLITA.   One thing more.   55
  That you may know my single charity,
  Freely I here remit all interest
  I e'er could claim, and give you back your vows;
  And to confirm't—reach me a cup of wine—
  My Lord Soranzo, in this draught I drink   60
  Long rest t'ee! —Look to it, Vasques.

VASQUES.
  Fear nothing.   *He gives her a poison'd cup: she drinks.*

SORANZO.
  Hippolita, I thank you, and will pledge
  This happy union as another life;
  Wine, there!   65

VASQUES.
  You shall have none, neither shall you pledge her.

HIPPOLITA.
  How!

VASQUES.
  Know now, Mistress She-Devil, your own mischievous
  treachery hath kill'd you; I must not marry you.

HIPPOLITA.
  Villain!   70

OMNES.
  What's the matter?

VASQUES.
  Foolish woman, thou art now like a firebrand that hath
  kindled others and burnt thyself; *troppo sperar, inganna,*

68–69.] *Weber;* Know ... treachery/   73. *inganna*] *Weber; niganna Q.*
Hath ... marry you. *Q.*

---

55. *engag'd*] put under an obligation.
56. *single*] sincere, single-minded.
73. *troppo . . . inganna*] too much hope deceives.

thy vain hope hath deceived thee, thou art but dead; if
thou hast any grace, pray.   75

HIPPOLITA.

   Monster!

VASQUES.

   Die in charity, for shame! This thing of malice, this
woman, had privately corrupted me with promise of
marriage, under this politic reconciliation, to poison
my lord, whiles she might laugh at his confusion on his   80
marriage day. I promis'd her fair, but I knew what my
reward should have been; and would willingly have
spar'd her life, but that I was acquainted with the danger
of her disposition, and now have fitted her a just payment
in her own coin. There she is, she hath yet——and end   85
thy days in peace, vile woman; as for life there's no hope,
think not on't.

OMNES.

   Wonderful justice!

RICHARDETTO.   Heaven, thou art righteous.

HIPPOLITA.

   O, 'tis true;
I feel my minute coming. Had that slave   90
Kept promise (O, my torment!), thou this hour
Hadst died, Soranzo—heat above hell fire!—
Yet ere I pass away—cruel, cruel flames!—
Take here my curse amongst you; may thy bed
Of marriage be a rack unto thy heart,   95
Burn blood and boil in vengeance—O my heart,
My flame's intolerable!—Mayst thou live
To father bastards, may her womb bring forth
Monsters, and die together in your sins,
Hated, scorn'd, and unpitied!—O!—O!—   *Dies.*   100

FLORIO.

   Was e'er so vile a creature?

---

79. marriage] *Dodsley;* malice Q.   85. yet——and] *printed thus in Q.*

---

79. *politic*] cunning, hypocritical.
85. *yet——and*] Some words may have dropped from the text here, or
possibly "yet" is a misprint for "that" or "it" (Hippolita's punishment).

RICHARDETTO.   Here's the end
  Of lust and pride.
ANNABELLA.   It is a fearful sight.
SORANZO.
  Vasques, I know thee now a trusty servant,
  And never will forget thee. —Come, my love,
  We'll home, and thank the Heavens for this escape.   105
  Father and friends, we must break up this mirth;
  It is too sad a feast.
DONADO.   Bear hence the body.
FRIAR.
  Here's an ominous change;
  Mark this, my Giovanni, and take heed.
  I fear the event; that marriage seldom's good,   110
  Where the bride-banquet so begins in blood.   *Exeunt.*

[IV.ii]   *Enter* Richardetto *and* Philotis.

RICHARDETTO.
  My wretched wife, more wretched in her shame
  Than in her wrongs to me, hath paid too soon
  The forfeit of her modesty and life;
  And I am sure, my niece, though vengeance hover,
  Keeping aloof yet from Soranzo's fall,   5
  Yet he will fall, and sink with his own weight.
  I need not now—my heart persuades me so—
  To further his confusion; there is One
  Above begins to work, for, as I hear,
  Debates already 'twixt his wife and him   10
  Thicken and run to head; she, as 'tis said,
  Slightens his love, and he abandons hers.
  Much talk I hear; since things go thus, my niece,
  In tender love and pity of your youth,
  My counsel is, that you should free your years   15
  From hazard of these woes by flying hence
  To fair Cremona, there to vow your soul
  In holiness a holy votaress:
  Leave me to see the end of these extremes.
  All human worldly courses are uneven;   20
  No life is blessed but the way to Heaven.

PHILOTIS.

Uncle, shall I resolve to be a nun?

RICHARDETTO.

Ay, gentle niece, and in your hourly prayers
Remember me, your poor unhappy uncle.
Hie to Cremona now, as fortune leads,　　　　　　　25
Your home your cloister, your best friends your beads.
Your chaste and single life shall crown your birth;
Who dies a virgin lives a saint on earth.

PHILOTIS.

Then farewell, world, and worldly thoughts, adieu!
Welcome, chaste vows; myself I yield to you.　　*Exeunt.*　　30

[IV.iii]　　　*Enter* Soranzo *unbrac'd, and* Annabella *dragg'd in.*

SORANZO.

Come, strumpet, famous whore! Were every drop
Of blood that runs in thy adulterous veins
A life, this sword—dost see't?—should in one blow
Confound them all. Harlot, rare, notable harlot,
That with thy brazen face maintainst thy sin,　　　　5
Was there no man in Parma to be bawd
To your loose cunning whoredom else but I?
Must your hot itch and pleurisy of lust,
The heyday of your luxury, be fed
Up to a surfeit, and could none but I　　　　　　10
Be pick'd out to be cloak to your close tricks,
Your belly-sports? Now I must be the dad
To all that gallimaufry that's stuff'd
In thy corrupted bastard-bearing womb,
Say, must I?

28. lives] *Dodsley;* live *Q*.　　　　　　[IV.iii]
　　　　　　　　　　　　　　　　15. Say] *Dodsley;* Shey *Q*.

0.1. *unbrac'd*] with part of his clothing untied; a symbol of mental turmoil
(cf. *Hamlet*, II.i.78).
　5. *maintainst*] defend, persist in.
　9. *luxury*] lust, lechery.
　11. *close*] secret, concealed.
　13. *gallimaufry*] an unpleasant mixture.

ANNABELLA.   Beastly man! Why, 'tis thy fate.   15
I sued not to thee; for, but that I thought
Your over-loving lordship would have run
Mad on denial, had ye lent me time,
I would have told 'ee in what case I was.
But you would needs be doing.
SORANZO.   Whore of whores!   20
Dar'st thou tell me this?
ANNABELLA.   O yes, why not?
You were deceiv'd in me; 'twas not for love
I chose you, but for honor; yet know this,
Would you be patient yet, and hide your shame,
I'd see whether I could love you.
SORANZO.   Excellent quean!   25
Why, art thou not with child?
ANNABELLA.   What needs all this
When 'tis superfluous? I confess I am.
SORANZO.
Tell me by whom.
ANNABELLA.   Soft, sir, 'twas not in my bargain.
Yet somewhat, sir, to stay your longing stomach,
I'm content t'acquaint you with; the man,   30
The more than man, that got this sprightly boy—
For 'tis a boy; that's for your glory, sir,
Your heir shall be a son—
SORANZO.   Damnable monster!
ANNABELLA.
Nay, and you will not hear, I'll speak no more.
SORANZO.
Yes, speak, and speak thy last.
ANNABELLA.   A match, a match!   35
This noble creature was in every part
So angel-like, so glorious, that a woman
Who had not been but human, as was I,
Would have kneel'd to him, and have begg'd for love.

32. that's for your] *McIlwraith;* that
for *Q;* and therefore *Dodsley.*

25. *quean*] impudent woman, harlot.
35. *A match*] i.e., a bargain! agreed!

You! Why, you are not worthy once to name   40
His name without true worship, or, indeed,
Unless you kneel'd, to hear another name him.
SORANZO.
    What was he call'd?
ANNABELLA.   We are not come to that.
    Let it suffice that you shall have the glory
    To father what so brave a father got.   45
    In brief, had not this chance fall'n out as't doth,
    I never had been troubled with a thought
    That you had been a creature; but for marriage,
    I scarce dream yet of that.
SORANZO.
    Tell me his name.
ANNABELLA.
                    Alas, alas, there's all!   50
    Will you believe?
SORANZO.   What?
ANNABELLA.   You shall never know.
SORANZO.
    How!
ANNABELLA. Never; if you do, let me be curs'd.
SORANZO.
    Not know it, strumpet! I'll rip up thy heart,
    And find it there.
ANNABELLA.   Do, do!
SORANZO.   And with my teeth
    Tear the prodigious lecher joint by joint.   55
ANABELLA.
    Ha, ha, ha, the man's merry!
SORANZO.   Dost thou laugh?
    Come, whore, tell me your lover, or, by truth,
    I'll hew thy flesh to shreds; who is't?
ANNABELLA (*sings*).
    Che morte piu dolce che morire per amore?
SORANZO.
    Thus will I pull thy hair, and thus I'll drag   60

52. Never . . . curs'd] *this   edn.;*   59. *piu*] *Weber; pluis* Q.
Never;/ If . . . curs'd. *Q.*

---

59. *Che . . . amore?*] "What sweeter death than to die for love?"

Thy lust-be-leper'd body through the dust.
Yet tell his name.
ANNABELLA (*sings*).
Morendo in gratia Dei, morirei senza dolore.
SORANZO.
Dost thou triumph? The treasure of the earth
Shall not redeem thee; were there kneeling kings   65
Did beg thy life, or angels did come down
To plead in tears, yet should not all prevail
Against my rage! Dost thou not tremble yet?
ANNABELLA.
At what? To die? No, be a gallant hangman.
I dare thee to the worst: strike, and strike home;   70
I leave revenge behind, and thou shalt feel't.
SORANZO.
Yet tell me ere thou diest, and tell me truly,
Knows thy old father this?
ANNABELLA.   No, by my life.
SORANZO.
Wilt thou confess, and I will spare thy life?
ANNABELLA.
My life! I will not buy my life so dear.   75
SORANZO.
I will not slack my vengeance.

                    Enter Vasques.

VASQUES.
What d'ee mean, sir?
SORANZO.
Forbear, Vasques; such a damned whore
Deserves no pity.

63. *Dei*] Weber; *Lei* Q.   71. I leave] Q *corr.;* leave Q *uncorr.*
63. *morirei*] *this edn.; morirere* Q *corr.;*
morire Q *uncorr.*

---

61. *lust-be-leper'd*] made leprous and repulsive through lust.
63. *Morendo . . . dolore*] A mixture of Italian and Latin: "Dying in the grace of God, I should die without sorrow." The reading *morirei* seems the most economical way of making sense of Q, but it is hard to explain why the compositor made the mistaken correction to *morirere*; obviously he did not understand Italian. Annabella's two lines in Italian are presumably quotations, but no editor has identified them.

VASQUES.

 Now the gods forfend! And would you be her executioner, 80
and kill her in your rage too? O, 'twere most unmanlike.
She is your wife: what faults hath been done by her before
she married you, were not against you; alas, poor lady, what
hath she committed which any lady in Italy in the like case
would not? Sir, you must be ruled by your reason and 85
not by your fury, that were unhuman and beastly.

SORANZO.

 She shall not live.

VASQUES.

 Come, she must. You would have her confess the author
of her present misfortunes, I warrant'ee; 'tis an unconscion-
able demand, and she should lose the estimation that I, 90
for my part, hold of her worth, if she had done it. Why,
sir, you ought not of all men living to know it: good sir,
be reconciled; alas, good gentlewoman!

ANNABELLA.

 Pish, do not beg for me: I prize my life
As nothing; if the man will needs be mad, 95
Why, let him take it.

SORANZO.   Vasques, hear'st thou this?

VASQUES.

 Yes, and commend her for it; in this she shows the nobleness
of a gallant spirit, and beshrew my heart, but it becomes her
rarely. [*Aside to* Soranzo.] Sir, in any case smother
your revenge; leave the scenting-out your wrongs to me; 100
be rul'd, as you respect your honor, or you mar all. [*Aloud.*]
Sir, if ever my service were of any credit with you, be not so
violent in your distractions. You are married now; what a
triumph might the report of this give to other neglected
suitors! 'Tis as manlike to bear extremities as godlike to 105
forgive.

SORANZO.

 O Vasques, Vasques, in this piece of flesh,
This faithless face of hers, had I laid up
The treasure of my heart! —Hadst thou been virtuous,

88. author] *Dyce;* authors *Q.*

---

80. *forfend*] forbid.

Fair, wicked woman, not the matchless joys   110
Of life itself had made me wish to live
With any saint but thee; deceitful creature,
How hast thou mock'd my hopes, and in the shame
Of thy lewd womb even buried me alive!
I did too dearly love thee.   115

VASQUES (*aside*).

This is well; follow this temper with some passion. Be brief
and moving; 'tis for the purpose.

SORANZO.

Be witness to my words thy soul and thoughts,
And tell me, didst not think that in my heart
I did too superstitiously adore thee?   120

ANNABELLA.

I must confess I know you lov'd me well.

SORANZO.

And wouldst thou use me thus? O, Annabella,
Be thou assur'd, whatsoe'er the villain was
That thus hath tempted thee to this disgrace,
Well he might lust, but never lov'd like me.   125
He doted on the picture that hung out
Upon thy cheeks, to please his humorous eye;
Not on the part I lov'd, which was thy heart,
And, as I thought, thy virtues.

ANNABELLA.   O my lord!

These words wound deeper than your sword could do. 130

VASQUES.

Let me not ever take comfort, but I begin to weep myself,
so much I pity him; why, madam, I knew when his rage was
over-past, what it would come to.

SORANZO.

Forgive me, Annabella: though thy youth

116–117.] *Weber;* This . . . well;/   123. thou] *Gifford;* thus *Q.*
Follow . . . passion./ Be . . . purpose.
Q.

---

116. *follow . . . passion*] i.e., go on talking in this way, with plenty of
feeling; it is the right way to trick Annabella into confessing.
127. *humorous*] capricious.

Hath tempted thee above thy strength to folly,   135
Yet will not I forget what I should be,
And what I am, a husband; in that name
Is hid divinity; if I do find
That thou wilt yet be true, here I remit
All former faults, and take thee to my bosom.   140

VASQUES.

By my troth, and that's a point of noble charity.

ANNABELLA.

Sir, on my knees—   [*Kneels.*]

SORANZO.   Rise up, you shall not kneel.
Get you to your chamber, see you make no show
Of alteration; I'll be with you straight.
My reason tells me now that 'tis as common   145
To err in frailty as to be a woman.
Go to your chamber.   *Exit* Annabella.

VASQUES.

So, this was somewhat to the matter; what do you think
of your heaven of happiness now, sir?

SORANZO.

I carry hell about me; all my blood   150
Is fir'd in swift revenge.

VASQUES.

That may be, but know you how, or on whom? Alas, to
marry a great woman, being made great in the stock to
your hand, is a usual sport in these days; but to know
what ferret it was that haunted your cony-berry, there's   155
the cunning.

SORANZO.

I'll make her tell herself, or—

VASQUES.

Or what? You must not do so. Let me yet persuade your
sufferance a little while; go to her, use her mildly, win her

---

155. ferret] *Dodsley;* secret *Q.*

153. *great*] pregnant.
153. *stock*] trunk, body.
153–154. *to your hand*] ready for you, in advance.
155. *cony-berry*] rabbit-warren.

if it be possible to a voluntary, to a weeping tune; for the 160
rest, if all hit, I will not miss my mark. Pray, sir, go in; the
next news I tell you shall be wonders.

SORANZO.

Delay in vengeance gives a heavier blow.   *Exit.*

VASQUES.

Ah, sirrah, here’s work for the nonce! I had a suspicion
of a bad matter in my head a pretty whiles ago; but after 165
my madam’s scurvy looks here at home, her waspish
perverseness and loud fault-finding, then I remember’d
the proverb, that where hens crow and cocks hold their
peace there are sorry houses. ’Sfoot, if the lower parts of a
she-tailor’s cunning can cover such a swelling in the   170
stomach, I’ll never blame a false stitch in a shoe whiles I
live again. Up and up so quick? And so quickly too?
’Twere a fine policy to learn by whom this must be known;
and I have thought on’t—Here’s the way, or none.

Enter Putana.

What, crying, old mistress! Alas, alas, I cannot blame ’ee, 175
we have a lord, Heaven help us, is so mad as the devil
himself, the more shame for him.

PUTANA.

O Vasques, that ever I was born to see this day! Doth he
use thee so too, sometimes, Vasques?

VASQUES.

Me? Why, he makes a dog of me. But if some were of my 180
mind, I know what we would do; as sure as I am an honest
man, he will go near to kill my lady with unkindness.
Say she be with child, is that such a matter for a young
woman of her years to be blam’d for?

PUTANA.

Alas, good heart, it is against her will full sore.   185

VASQUES.

I durst be sworn, all his madness is for that she will not
confess whose ’tis, which he will know, and when he doth

174.1.] *Weber; after l. 177 in* Q.

---

160. *voluntary*] a pun: (1) an extempore or improvised piece of music;
(2) a spontaneous confession.
168–169. *where . . . houses*] proverbial; cf. Tilley, H 778.

know it, I am so well acquainted with his humor, that he
will forget all straight. Well, I could wish she would in
plain terms tell all, for that's the way indeed.   190

PUTANA.

Do you think so?

VASQUES.

Foh, I know't; provided that he did not win her to't by
force. He was once in a mind that you could tell, and
meant to have wrung it out of you, but I somewhat pacified
him for that; yet sure you know a great deal.   195

PUTANA.

Heaven forgive us all! I know a little, Vasques.

VASQUES.

Why should you not? Who else should? Upon my conscience,
she loves you dearly, and you would not betray her to any
affliction for the world.

PUTANA.

Not for all the world, by my faith and troth, Vasques.   200

VASQUES.

'Twere pity of your life if you should, but in this you
should both relieve her present discomforts, pacify my
lord, and gain yourself everlasting love and preferment.

PUTANA.

Dost think so, Vasques?

VASQUES.

Nay, I know't; sure 'twas some near and entire friend.   205

PUTANA.

'Twas a dear friend indeed; but—

VASQUES.

But what? Fear not to name him; my life between you and
danger. Faith, I think 'twas no base fellow.

PUTANA.

Thou wilt stand between me and harm?

VASQUES.

'Ud's pity, what else? You shall be rewarded too, trust me. 210

PUTANA.

'Twas even no worse than her own brother.

---

210. *'Ud's*] God's.

VASQUES.

Her brother Giovanni, I warrant ’ee!

PUTANA.

Even he, Vasques; as brave a gentleman as ever kiss’d fair
lady. O, they love most perpetually!

VASQUES.

A brave gentleman indeed; why, therein I commend her 215
choice. —Better and better! —You are sure ’twas he?

PUTANA.

Sure; and you shall see he will not be long from her too.

VASQUES.

He were to blame if he would: but may I believe thee?

PUTANA.

Believe me! Why, dost think I am a Turk or a Jew? No,
Vasques, I have known their dealings too long to belie 220
them now.

VASQUES.

Where are you there? Within, sirs!

Enter Banditti.

PUTANA.

How now, what are these?

VASQUES.

You shall know presently. Come, sirs, take me this old
damnable hag, gag her instantly, and put out her eyes. 225
Quickly, quickly!

PUTANA.

Vasques, Vasques!

VASQUES.

Gag her, I say! ’Sfoot, d’ee suffer her to prate? What d’ee
fumble about? Let me come to her; I’ll help your old
gums, you toad-bellied bitch. Sirs, carry her closely into the 230
coalhouse, and put out her eyes instantly; if she roars, slit her
nose: d’ee hear, be speedy and sure. Why, this is excellent
and above expectation.   *Exeunt* [Banditti] *with* Putana.

224–226.] *Weber;* You ... presently./   233. S.D. *Exeunt*] *Dodsley; Exit Q.*
Come ... hag,/ Gag ... quickly! *Q.*

224. *presently*] immediately.

Her own brother! O horrible! To what a height of liberty
in damnation hath the devil train'd our age, her brother! 235
Well, there's yet but a beginning: I must to my lord, and
tutor him better in his points of vengeance; now I see
how a smooth tale goes beyond a smooth tail. But soft—
What thing comes next?

Enter Giovanni.

Giovanni! As I would wish; my belief is strengthen'd, 240
'tis as firm as winter and summer.

GIOVANNI.

Where's my sister?

VASQUES.

Troubled with a new sickness, my lord; she's somewhat
ill.

GIOVANNI.

Took too much of the flesh, I believe.   245

VASQUES.

Troth, sir, and you, I think, have e'en hit it. But my
virtuous lady—

GIOVANNI.

Where's she?

VASQUES.

In her chamber; please you visit her; she is alone.
[Giovanni *gives him money*.] Your liberality hath doubly 250
made me your servant, and ever shall, ever.

                                     Exit Giovanni.

Enter Soranzo.

Sir, I am made a man, I have plied my cue with cunning
and success; I beseech you let's be private.

SORANZO.

My lady's brother's come; now he'll know all.

VASQUES.

Let him know't; I have made some of them fast enough. 255

246–247.] *Weber;* Troth . . . it./ But
. . . lady—*Q*.

---

234. *liberty*] license, libertinage.
235. *train'd*] lured, enticed.
245. *Took . . . flesh*] a bawdy double meaning: (1) eaten too much meat;
(2) had too much sexual experience and become pregnant.

How have you dealt with my lady?

SORANZO.

    Gently, as thou hast counsel'd. O, my soul
    Runs circular in sorrow for revenge!
    But, Vasques, thou shalt know—

VASQUES.

    Nay, I will know no more, for now comes your turn to 260
    know; I would not talk so openly with you. Let my young
    master take time enough, and go at pleasure; he is sold to
    death, and the devil shall not ransom him. Sir, I beseech
    you, your privacy.

SORANZO.

    No conquest can gain glory of my fear.   *Exeunt.* 265

[V.i]   *Enter* Annabella *above.*

ANNABELLA.

    Pleasures, farewell, and all ye thriftless minutes
    Wherein false joys have spun a weary life!
    To these my fortunes now I take my leave.
    Thou, precious Time, that swiftly rid'st in post
    Over the world, to finish up the race   5
    Of my last fate, here stay thy restless course,
    And bear to ages that are yet unborn
    A wretched, woeful woman's tragedy.
    My conscience now stands up against my lust
    With depositions character'd in guilt,   10

            Enter Friar [*below*].

    And tells me I am lost: now I confess
    Beauty that clothes the outside of the face
    Is cursed if it be not cloth'd with grace.
    Here like a turtle mew'd up in a cage,

265. S.D. *Exeunt*] Dodsley; *Exit Q.*   [V.i]
                           10. depositions] *Dodsley;* dispositions
                           Q.

---

    9. *against*] as a witness against.
    10. *depositions*] This seems to fit the legal metaphor better than the reading of *Q.*
    10. *character'd in guilt*] Apparently a punning phrase: (1) with gilt lettering; (2) written so as to expose Annabella's guilt.
    14. *turtle*] turtle-dove.

Unmated, I converse with air and walls,   15
And descant on my vile unhappiness.
O Giovanni, that hast had the spoil
Of thine own virtues and my modest fame,
Would thou hadst been less subject to those stars
That luckless reign'd at my nativity: 20
O would the scourge due to my black offense
Might pass from thee, that I alone might feel
The torment of an uncontrolled flame!

FRIAR [*aside*].
    What's this I hear?

ANNABELLA.   That man, that blessed friar,
Who join'd in ceremonial knot my hand   25
To him whose wife I now am, told me oft
I trod the path to death, and showed me how.
But they who sleep in lethargies of lust
Hug their confusion, making Heaven unjust,
And so did I.

FRIAR [*aside*].   Here's music to the soul!   30

ANNABELLA.
    Forgive me, my good genius, and this once
Be helpful to my ends; let some good man
Pass this way, to whose trust I may commit
This paper double-lin'd with tears and blood:
Which being granted, here I sadly vow   35
Repentance, and a leaving of that life
I long have died in.

FRIAR.   Lady, Heaven hath heard you,
And hath by providence ordain'd that I
Should be his minister for your behoof.

ANNABELLA.
    Ha, what are you?

FRIAR.   Your brother's friend, the friar;   40
Glad in my soul that I have liv'd to hear
This free confession 'twixt your peace and you.
What would you, or to whom? Fear not to speak.

ANNABELLA.
    Is Heaven so bountiful? Then I have found

---

35. *sadly*] seriously.

More favor than I hop'd. Here, holy man—   45

Throws a letter.

Commend me to my brother; give him that,
That letter; bid him read it and repent.
Tell him that I, imprison'd in my chamber,
Barr'd of all company, even of my guardian,
Who gives me cause of much suspect, have time   50
To blush at what hath pass'd; bid him be wise,
And not believe the friendship of my lord.
I fear much more than I can speak: good father,
The place is dangerous, and spies are busy;
I must break off—you'll do't?

FRIAR.   Be sure I will;   55
And fly with speed—my blessing ever rest
With thee, my daughter: live, to die more blessed!

Exit Friar.

ANNABELLA.

Thanks to the Heavens, who have prolong'd my breath
To this good use: now I can welcome death.   *Exit.*

[V.ii]   *Enter* Soranzo *and* Vasques.

VASQUES.

Am I to be believ'd now? First marry a strumpet that cast
herself away upon you but to laugh at your horns, to feast
on your disgrace, riot in your vexations, cuckold you in
your bride-bed, waste your estate upon panders and bawds!

SORANZO.

No more, I say, no more!   5

VASQUES.

A cuckold is a goodly tame beast, my lord.

SORANZO.

I am resolv'd; urge not another word.
My thoughts are great, and all as resolute
As thunder; in mean time I'll cause our lady
To deck herself in all her bridal robes,   10
Kiss her, and fold her gently in my arms.

---

50. *suspect*] suspicion.

Begone—yet hear you, are the banditti ready
To wait in ambush?

VASQUES.

Good sir, trouble not yourself about other business than
your own resolution; remember that time lost cannot be   15
recall'd.

SORANZO.

With all the cunning words thou canst, invite
The states of Parma to my birthday's feast;
Haste to my brother-rival and his father,
Entreat them gently, bid them not to fail.   20
Be speedy, and return.

VASQUES.

Let not your pity betray you till my coming back; think upon
incest and cuckoldry.

SORANZO.

Revenge is all the ambition I aspire:
To that I'll climb or fall; my blood's on fire.   *Exeunt.* 25

[V.iii]   *Enter* Giovanni.

GIOVANNI.

Busy opinion is an idle fool,
That as a school-rod keeps a child in awe,
Frights the unexperienc'd temper of the mind:
So did it me; who, ere my precious sister
Was married, thought all taste of love would die   5
In such a contract; but I find no change
Of pleasure in this formal law of sports.
She is still one to me, and every kiss
As sweet and as delicious as the first
I reap'd, when yet the privilege of youth   10
Entitled her a virgin. O the glory
Of two united hearts like hers and mine!
Let poring book-men dream of other worlds,
My world, and all of happiness, is here,

---

18. *states*] people of importance, dignitaries.
[V.iii]
   1. *opinion*] what most people think; commonly-held beliefs.

And I'd not change it for the best to come: 15
A life of pleasure is Elysium.

Enter Friar.

Father, you enter on the jubilee
Of my retir'd delights; now I can tell you,
The hell you oft have prompted is nought else
But slavish and fond superstitious fear;   20
And I could prove it too—

FRIAR.   Thy blindness slays thee.
Look there, 'tis writ to thee.   *Gives the letter.*

GIOVANNI.
From whom?

FRIAR.
Unrip the seals and see;
The blood's yet seething hot, that will anon   25
Be frozen harder than congeal'd coral.
Why d'ee change color, son?

GIOVANNI.   'Fore Heaven, you make
Some petty devil factor 'twixt my love
And your religion-masked sorceries.
Where had you this?

FRIAR.   Thy conscience, youth, is sear'd,   30
Else thou wouldst stoop to warning.

GIOVANNI.   'Tis her hand,
I know't; and 'tis all written in her blood.
She writes I know not what. Death? I'll not fear
An armed thunderbolt aim'd at my heart.
She writes, we are discovered—pox on dreams   35
Of low faint-hearted cowardice! Discovered?
The devil we are; which way is't possible?
Are we grown traitors to our own delights?
Confusion take such dotage, 'tis but forg'd;
This is your peevish chattering, weak old man.   40

Enter Vasques.

40.1] *Dyce; after l. 41 in Q.*

---

17. *jubilee*] This usually means "a time of rejoicing or celebration," but
its precise meaning at this point is not clear.
19. *prompted*] put forward (during arguments with Giovanni).
30. *sear'd*] dried or withered, incapable of feeling.

Now, sir, what news bring you?

VASQUES.

My lord, according to his yearly custom keeping this day a
feast in honor of his birthday, by me invites you thither.
Your worthy father, with the Pope's reverend nuncio, and
other magnificoes of Parma, have promis'd their presence;   45
will't please you to be of the number?

GIOVANNI.

Yes, tell him I dare come.

VASQUES.

"Dare come"?

GIOVANNI.

So I said; and tell him more, I will come.

VASQUES.

These words are strange to me.   50

GIOVANNI.

Say I will come.

VASQUES.

You will not miss?

GIOVANNI.

Yet more? I'll come! Sir, are you answer'd?

VASQUES.

So I'll say. —My service to you.   *Exit* Vasques.

FRIAR. You will not go, I trust.

GIOVANNI.   Not go! For what?   55

FRIAR.

O, do not go! This feast, I'll gage my life,
Is but a plot to train you to your ruin;
Be rul'd, you sha' not go.

GIOVANNI.   Not go? Stood Death
Threat'ning his armies of confounding plagues,
With hosts of dangers hot as blazing stars,   60
I would be there. Not go? Yes, and resolve
To strike as deep in slaughter as they all.
For I will go.

47. him] *Gifford;* them *Q*.

---

56. *gage*] pledge, wager.
57. *train*] lure.

FRIAR.   Go where thou wilt; I see
      The wildness of thy fate draws to an end,
      To a bad fearful end. I must not stay   65
      To know thy fall; back to Bononia I
      With speed will haste, and shun this coming blow.
      Parma, farewell; would I had never known thee,
      Or aught of thine! Well, young man, since no prayer
      Can make thee safe, I leave thee to despair.   *Exit* Friar. 70
GIOVANNI.
      Despair, or tortures of a thousand hells,
      All's one to me; I have set up my rest.
      Now, now, work serious thoughts on baneful plots,
      Be all a man, my soul; let not the curse
      Of old prescription rend from me the gall   75
      Of courage, which enrols a glorious death.
      If I must totter like a well-grown oak,
      Some under-shrubs shall in my weighty fall
      Be crush'd to splits: with me they all shall perish.   *Exit.*

[V.iv]   *Enter* Soranzo, Vasques, *and* Banditti.

SORANZO.
      You will not fail, or shrink in the attempt?
VASQUES.
      I will undertake for their parts. Be sure, my masters, to be
      bloody enough, and as unmerciful as if you were preying
      upon a rich booty on the very mountains of Liguria; for
      your pardons, trust to my lord, but for reward you shall   5
      trust none but your own pockets.
BANDITTI OMNES.
      We'll make a murder.

71. S.P. GIOVANNI] *Dodsley; omitted in*
Q.

72. *set up my rest*] a metaphor from the card-game of primero, in which the
player eventually stands or rests upon his hand of cards in the hope that it
will prove better than his opponent's.
75. *old prescription*] apparently a reference to the biblical commandments.
76. *enrols*] sets one's name in the lists or records of those who have died
bravely.
79. *splits*] splinters.

SORANZO.

Here's gold, here's more; want nothing; what you do
Is noble, and an act of brave revenge.
I'll make ye rich banditti, and all free.   10

OMNES.

Liberty, liberty!

VASQUES.

Hold, take every man a vizard; when ye are withdrawn,
keep as much silence as you can possibly. You know the
watchword; till which be spoken, move not, but when you
hear that, rush in like a stormy flood; I need not instruct   15
ye in your own profession.

OMNES.

No, no, no.

VASQUES.

In, then: your ends are profit and preferment. —Away!

                                              Exeunt Banditti.

SORANZO.

The guests will all come, Vasques?

VASQUES.

Yes, sir. And now let me a little edge your resolution. You   20
see nothing is unready to this great work, but a great mind
in you: call to your remembrance your disgraces, your
loss of honor, Hippolita's blood, and arm your courage
in your own wrongs; so shall you best right those wrongs
in vengeance, which you may truly call your own.   25

SORANZO.

'Tis well; the less I speak, the more I burn,
And blood shall quench that flame.

VASQUES.

Now you begin to turn Italian. This beside—when my
young incest-monger comes, he will be sharp set on his
old bit: give him time enough, let him have your chamber   30
and bed at liberty; let my hot hare have law ere he be

18.1. *Exeunt*] *Reed; Exit Q*.

---

29. *be . . . on*] have a hungry appetite for.
31. *law*] a "start," or limited freedom before the pursuit begins.

hunted to his death, that if it be possible, he may post to
hell in the very act of his damnation.

Enter Giovanni.

SORANZO.
It shall be so; and see, as we would wish,
He comes himself first. Welcome, my much-lov'd brother!   35
Now I perceive you honor me; y'are welcome.
But where's my father?
GIOVANNI.   With the other states,
Attending on the nuncio of the Pope,
To wait upon him hither. How's my sister?
SORANZO.
Like a good housewife, scarcely ready yet;   40
Y'are best walk to her chamber.
GIOVANNI.   If you will.
SORANZO.
I must expect my honorable friends;
Good brother, get her forth.
GIOVANNI.   You are busy, sir.

Exit Giovanni.

VASQUES.
Even as the great devil himself would have it; let him go
and glut himself in his own destruction.   *Flourish.*   45
Hark, the nuncio is at hand; good sir, be ready to receive
him.

Enter Cardinal, Florio, Donado, Richardetto, *and Attendants.*

SORANZO.
Most reverend lord, this grace hath made me proud,
That you vouchsafe my house; I ever rest
Your humble servant for this noble favor.   50

---

45. S.D. *Flourish*] *Q uncorr.; after l. 47,*
Q corr.   (correction made in error by proof-
reader).

32–33. *post . . . damnation*] If he is killed in the middle of a sinful act, his soul
will be damned as well as his body destroyed. This refinement of vengeance
is mentioned in *Hamlet* (III.iii) and several other early seventeenth-century
plays.
42. *expect*] await.
49. *vouchsafe*] deign to visit.

CARDINAL.

    You are our friend, my lord; his Holiness
    Shall understand how zealously you honor
    Saint Peter's vicar in his substitute.
    Our special love to you.

SORANZO.   Signors, to you

    My welcome, and my ever best of thanks   55
    For this so memorable courtesy.
    Pleaseth your grace to walk near?

CARDINAL.   My lord, we come

    To celebrate your feast with civil mirth,
    As ancient custom teacheth: we will go.

SORANZO.

    Attend his grace there! Signors, keep your way.   *Exeunt.*   60

[V.v]   *Enter* Giovanni *and* Annabella *lying on a bed.*

GIOVANNI.

    What, chang'd so soon? Hath your new sprightly lord
    Found out a trick in night-games more than we
    Could know in our simplicity? Ha! Is't so?
    Or does the fit come on you, to prove treacherous
    To your past vows and oaths?

ANNABELLA.   Why should you jest   5

    At my calamity, without all sense
    Of the approaching dangers you are in?

GIOVANNI.

    What danger's half so great as thy revolt?
    Thou art a faithless sister, else thou know'st
    Malice, or any treachery beside,   10
    Would stoop to my bent brows; why, I hold fate
    Clasp'd in my fist, and could command the course
    Of time's eternal motion, hadst thou been
    One thought more steady than an ebbing sea.
    And what? You'll now be honest, that's resolv'd?   15

ANNABELLA.

    Brother, dear brother, know what I have been,

0.1 *Enter . . . bed*] The bed may have been pushed out onto the stage; compare the S.D. in Middleton's *A Chaste Maid in Cheapside*, III.ii: "*A bed thrust out upon the stage; Allwit's wife in it.*"

And know that now there's but a dining-time
'Twixt us and our confusion: let's not waste
These precious hours in vain and useless speech.
Alas, these gay attires were not put on   20
But to some end; this sudden solemn feast
Was not ordain'd to riot in expense;
I, that have now been chamber'd here alone,
Barr'd of my guardian, or of any else,
Am not for nothing at an instant freed   25
To fresh access. Be not deceiv'd, my brother:
This banquet is an harbinger of death
To you and me; resolve yourself it is,
And be prepar'd to welcome it.
GIOVANNI.   Well, then;
The schoolmen teach that all this globe of earth   30
Shall be consum'd to ashes in a minute.
ANNABELLA.
So I have read too.
GIOVANNI.   But 'twere somewhat strange
To see the waters burn: could I believe
This might be true, I could believe as well
There might be hell or Heaven.
ANNABELLA.   That's most certain.   35
GIOVANNI.
A dream, a dream! Else in this other world
We should know one another.
ANNABELLA.   So we shall.
GIOVANNI.
Have you heard so?
ANNABELLA.   For certain.
GIOVANNI.   But d'ee think
That I shall see you there? —You look on me?
May we kiss one another, prate or laugh,   40
Or do as we do here?
ANNABELLA.   I know not that.
But good, for the present, what d'ee mean

17. dining] Q corr.; dying Q uncorr.   39–40.] Dodsley; That . . . there,/
                                          You . . . me?/   May . . . another,/
                                          Prate or laugh, Q.

30. schoolmen] medieval theologians.

    To free yourself from danger? Some way think
    How to escape; I'm sure the guests are come.

GIOVANNI.
    Look up, look here; what see you in my face?   45

ANNABELLA.
    Distraction and a troubled countenance.

GIOVANNI.
    Death, and a swift repining wrath—yet look,
    What see you in mine eyes?

ANNABELLA.   Methinks you weep.

GIOVANNI.
    I do indeed; these are the funeral tears
    Shed on your grave; these furrowed up my cheeks   50
    When first I lov'd and knew not how to woo.
    Fair Annabella, should I here repeat
    The story of my life, we might lose time.
    Be record all the spirits of the air,
    And all things else that are, that day and night,   55
    Early and late, the tribute which my heart
    Hath paid to Annabella's sacred love
    Hath been these tears, which are her mourners now.
    Never till now did Nature do her best
    To show a matchless beauty to the world,   60
    Which in an instant, ere it scarce was seen,
    The jealous Destinies requir'd again.
    Pray, Annabella, pray; since we must part,
    Go thou, white in thy soul, to fill a throne
    Of innocence and sanctity in Heaven.   65
    Pray, pray, my sister!

ANNABELLA.   Then I see your drift—
    Ye blessed angels, guard me!

GIOVANNI.   So say I.
    Kiss me; if ever after-times should hear
    Of our fast-knit affections, though perhaps
    The laws of conscience and of civil use   70
    May justly blame us, yet when they but know
    Our loves, that love will wipe away that rigor

51. woo] *Q corr.;* woe *Q uncorr.*   62. requir'd] *Q corr.;* require *Q.*
                                                  uncorr.

Which would in other incests be abhorr'd.
Give me your hand; how sweetly life doth run
In these well-colored veins! How constantly   75
These palms do promise health! But I could chide
With Nature for this cunning flattery.
Kiss me again—forgive me.

ANNABELLA.   With my heart.

GIOVANNI.
    Farewell.

ANNABELLA.   Will you be gone?

GIOVANNI.   Be dark, bright sun,
And make this midday night, that thy gilt rays   80
May not behold a deed will turn their splendor
More sooty than the poets feign their Styx!
One other kiss, my sister.

ANNABELLA.   What means this?

GIOVANNI.
    To save thy fame, and kill thee in a kiss.   *Stabs her.*
    Thus die, and die by me, and by my hand!   85
    Revenge is mine; honor doth love command.

ANNABELLA.
    O brother, by your hand?

GIOVANNI.   When thou art dead
I'll give my reasons for't; for to dispute
With thy (even in thy death) most lovely beauty,
Would make me stagger to perform this act,   90
Which I most glory in.

ANNABELLA.
    Forgive him, Heaven—and me my sins; farewell.
    Brother unkind, unkind!—Mercy, great Heaven—O!—O!—
                                              Dies.

GIOVANNI.
    She's dead, alas, good soul! The hapless fruit
    That in her womb receiv'd its life from me   95
    Hath had from me a cradle and a grave.
    I must not dally. This sad marriage-bed,
    In all her best, bore her alive and dead.
    Soranzo, thou hast miss'd thy aim in this;

---

93. *unkind*] used here with two meanings: (1) harsh, cruel; (2) unnatural.

I have prevented now thy reaching plots,   100
And kill'd a love, for whose each drop of blood
I would have pawn'd my heart. Fair Annabella,
How over-glorious art thou in thy wounds,
Triumphing over infamy and hate!
Shrink not, courageous hand, stand up, my heart,   105
And boldly act my last and greater part.

                                  Exit with the body.

[V.vi]

A Banquet. Enter Cardinal, Florio, Donado, Soranzo, Richardetto,
Vasques, *and Attendants; they take their places.*

VASQUES.

    Remember, sir, what you have to do, be wise and resolute.

SORANZO.

    Enough—my heart is fix'd. —Pleaseth your grace
To taste these coarse confections; though the use
Of such set entertainments more consists
In custom than in cause, yet, reverend sir,   5
I am still made your servant by your presence.

CARDINAL.

    And we your friend.

SORANZO.

    But where's my brother Giovanni?

           Enter Giovanni *with a heart upon his dagger.*

GIOVANNI.

    Here, here, Soranzo; trimm'd in reeking blood,
That triumphs over death; proud in the spoil   10
Of love and vengeance! Fate or all the powers
That guide the motions of immortal souls
Could not prevent me.

CARDINAL.

    What means this?

FLORIO.

    Son Giovanni!   15

---

100. *prevented*] forestalled, anticipated.
100. *reaching*] far-reaching, cunning.

SORANZO.

Shall I be forestall'd?

GIOVANNI.

Be not amaz'd; if your misgiving hearts
Shrink at an idle sight, what bloodless fear
Of coward passion would have seiz'd your senses,
Had you beheld the rape of life and beauty   20
Which I have acted? My sister, O my sister!

FLORIO.

Ha! What of her?

GIOVANNI.   The glory of my deed
Darken'd the midday sun, made noon as night.
You came to feast, my lords, with dainty fare;
I came to feast too, but I digg'd for food   25
In a much richer mine than gold or stone
Of any value balanc'd; 'tis a heart,
A heart, my lords, in which is mine entomb'd:
Look well upon't; d'ee know't?

VASQUES.

What strange riddle's this?   30

GIOVANNI.

'Tis Annabella's heart, 'tis; why d'ee startle?
I vow 'tis hers: this dagger's point plough'd up
Her fruitful womb, and left to me the fame
Of a most glorious executioner.

FLORIO.

Why, madman, art thyself?   35

GIOVANNI.

Yes, father; and that times to come may know
How as my fate I honor'd my revenge,
List, father, to your ears I will yield up
How much I have deserv'd to be your son.

FLORIO.

What is't thou say'st?

GIOVANNI.   Nine moons have had their changes   40
Since I first throughly view'd and truly lov'd
Your daughter and my sister.

FLORIO.   How! —Alas,
My lords, he's a frantic madman!

42–43. How . . . madman!] *McIl-*
wraith; one line in Q.

GIOVANNI.   Father, no.
    For nine months' space in secret I enjoy'd
    Sweet Annabella's sheets; nine months I liv'd   45
    A happy monarch of her heart and her.
    Soranzo, thou know'st this; thy paler cheek
    Bears the confounding print of thy disgrace,
    For her too fruitful womb too soon bewray'd
    The happy passage of our stol'n delights,   50
    And made her mother to a child unborn.

CARDINAL.
    Incestuous villain!

FLORIO.   O, his rage belies him.

GIOVANNI.
    It does not, 'tis the oracle of truth;
    I vow it is so.

SORANZO.   I shall burst with fury;
    Bring the strumpet forth!   55

VASQUES.
    I shall, sir.   *Exit* Vasques.

GIOVANNI.   Do, sir! Have you all no faith
    To credit yet my triumphs? Here I swear
    By all that you call sacred, by the love
    I bore my Annabella whilst she liv'd,
    These hands have from her bosom ripp'd this heart.   60

                Enter Vasques.
    Is't true or no, sir?

VASQUES.   'Tis most strangely true.

FLORIO.
    Cursed man! —Have I liv'd to—   *Dies.*

CARDINAL.   Hold up, Florio.
    Monster of children, see what thou hast done,
    Broke thy old father's heart! Is none of you
    Dares venture on him?

GIOVANNI.   Let 'em! O, my father,   65
    How well his death becomes him in his griefs!
    Why, this was done with courage; now survives
    None of our house but I, gilt in the blood
    Of a fair sister and a hapless father.

SORANZO.
    Inhuman scorn of men, hast thou a thought   70

T'outlive thy murders?

GIOVANNI.   Yes, I tell thee, yes;
For in my fists I bear the twists of life.
Soranzo, see this heart, which was thy wife's;
Thus I exchange it royally for thine,   [*Stabs him.*]
And thus and thus! Now brave revenge is mine.   75

VASQUES.
I cannot hold any longer. —You, sir, are you grown
insolent in your butcheries? Have at you!   [*They*] *fight.*

GIOVANNI.
Come, I am arm'd to meet thee.

VASQUES.
No, will it not be yet? If this will not, another shall. Not yet?
I shall fit you anon. —Vengeance!   80

Enter Banditti [*and fight* Giovanni].

GIOVANNI.
Welcome, come more of you whate'er you be,
I dare your worst—
O, I can stand no longer! Feeble arms,
Have you so soon lost strength?

VASQUES.
Now you are welcome, sir! —Away, my masters, all is done,   85
shift for yourselves! Your reward is your own; shift for
yourselves.

BANDITTI.
Away, away!   *Exeunt* Banditti.

VASQUES.
How d'ee, my lord; see you this? How is't?

SORANZO.
Dead; but in death well pleased that I have liv'd   90
To see my wrongs reveng'd on that black devil.

79–80.] *Dodsley;* No . . . shall./ Not   85–87.]   *Weber;*   Now . . . sir!/
. . . Vengeance! *Q.*   Away . . . done,/   Shift . . . own;/
                                             Shift for yourselves. *Q.*

---

72. *twists*] an allusion to the legend of the Fates or Parcae, who spun the
threads of man's life and cut them when they had reached the destined
length.
80. *fit you*] provide something that will cope with you.
80. *Vengeance!*] Presumably the watchword mentioned at V.iv.14.

O Vasques, to thy bosom let me give
My last of breath; let not that lecher live—O!—   *Dies.*

VASQUES.

The reward of peace and rest be with him, my ever dearest
lord and master.   95

GIOVANNI.

Whose hand gave me this wound?

VASQUES.

Mine, sir, I was your first man; have you enough?

GIOVANNI.

I thank thee; thou hast done for me but what
I would have else done on myself. Art sure
Thy lord is dead?   100

VASQUES.

O impudent slave! As sure as I am sure to see thee die.

CARDINAL.

Think on thy life and end, and call for mercy.

GIOVANNI.

Mercy? Why, I have found it in this justice.

CARDINAL.

Strive yet to cry to Heaven.

GIOVANNI.   O, I bleed fast.
Death, thou art a guest long look'd for; I embrace   105
Thee and thy wounds; O, my last minute comes!
Where'er I go, let me enjoy this grace,
Freely to view my Annabella's face.   *Dies.*

DONADO.

Strange miracle of justice!

CARDINAL

Raise up the city; we shall be murdered all!   110

VASQUES.

You need not fear, you shall not; this strange task being
ended, I have paid the duty to the son which I have vowed
to the father.

CARDINAL.

Speak, wretched villain, what incarnate fiend
Hath led thee on to this?   115

94–95.] *Weber;* The . . . him,/ My   98–100.] *this edn.; prose in* Q.
. . . master. Q.   101. thee] *Dodsley;* the Q.

VASQUES.

    Honesty, and pity of my master's wrongs; for know, my
lord, I am by birth a Spaniard, brought forth my country
in my youth by Lord Soranzo's father, whom whilst he
liv'd I serv'd faithfully; since whose death I have been
to this man as I was to him. What I have done was duty, 120
and I repent nothing but that the loss of my life had not
ransom'd his.

CARDINAL.

    Say, fellow, know'st thou any yet unnam'd
Of counsel in this incest?

VASQUES.

    Yes, an old woman, sometimes guardian to this murdered 125
lady.

CARDINAL.

    And what's become of her?

VASQUES.

    Within this room she is; whose eyes, after her confession, I
caus'd to be put out, but kept alive, to confirm what from
Giovanni's own mouth you have heard. Now, my lord, what 130
I have done you may judge of, and let your own wisdom be
a judge in your own reason.

CARDINAL.

    Peace! First this woman, chief in these effects:
My sentence is, that forthwith she be ta'en
Out of the city, for example's sake,   135
There to be burnt to ashes.

DONADO.   'Tis most just.

CARDINAL.

    Be it your charge, Donado, see it done.

DONADO.

    I shall.

VASQUES.

    What for me? If death, 'tis welcome; I have been honest
to the son as I was to the father.   140

CARDINAL.

    Fellow, for thee: since what thou didst was done

---

125. *sometimes*] formerly.

133. *this woman*] Most critics take this to refer to Putana, but the Cardinal
might possibly be thinking of the corpse of Annabella.

Not for thyself, being no Italian,
We banish thee forever, to depart
Within three days; in this we do dispense
With grounds of reason, not of thine offense.   145

VASQUES.
'Tis well; this conquest is mine, and I rejoice that a
Spaniard outwent an Italian in revenge.   *Exit* Vasques.

CARDINAL.
Take up these slaughtered bodies, see them buried;
And all the gold and jewels, or whatsoever
Confiscate by the canons of the church,   150
We seize upon to the Pope's proper use.

RICHARDETTO [*discovers himself*].
Your grace's pardon! thus long I liv'd disguis'd
To see the effect of pride and lust at once
Brought both to shameful ends.

CARDINAL.
What, Richardetto whom we thought for dead?   155

DONADO.
Sir, was it you—

RICHARDETTO.   Your friend.

CARDINAL.   We shall have time
To talk at large of all; but never yet
Incest and murder have so strangely met.
Of one so young, so rich in nature's store,
Who could not say, 'tis pity she's a whore?   *Exeunt.* 160

FINIS

The general commendation deserved by the actors in their presentment of this tragedy may easily excuse such few faults as are escaped in the printing. A common charity may allow him the ability of spelling whom a secure confidence assures that he cannot ignorantly err in the application of sense.

Appendix

Chronology

Approximate years are indicated by*, occurrences in doubt by (?).

Political and Literary Events	Life and Major Works of John Ford

1558
Accession of Queen Elizabeth I.
Robert Greene born.
Thomas Kyd born.

1560
George Chapman born.

1561
Francis Bacon born.

1564
Shakespeare born.
Christopher Marlowe born.

1570
Thomas Heywood born.*

1572
Thomas Dekker born.*
John Donne born.
Massacre of St. Bartholomew's Day.

1573
Ben Jonson born.

1576
The Theatre, the first permanent public theater in London, established by James Burbage.
John Marston born.

1577
The Curtain theater opened.
Holinshed's *Chronicles of England, Scotland and Ireland*.
Drake begins circumnavigation of

the earth; completed 1580.
1578
John Lyly's *Euphues: The Anatomy of Wit*.
1579
John Fletcher born.
Sir Thomas North's translation of Plutarch's *Lives*.
1580
Thomas Middleton born.
1583
Philip Massinger born.
1584
Francis Beaumont born.*
1586
Death of Sir Philip Sidney.   John Ford born at Ilsington, Devonshire, April 17.
1587
The Rose theater opened by Henslowe.
Marlowe's *TAMBURLAINE*, Part 1.*
Execution of Mary, Queen of Scots.
Drake raids Cadiz.
1588
Defeat of the Spanish Armada.
Marlowe's *TAMBURLAINE*, Part II.*
1589
Greene's *FRIAR BACON AND FRIAR BUNGAY*.*
Marlowe's *THE JEW OF MALTA*.*
Kyd's *THE SPANISH TRAGEDY*.*
1590
Spenser's *Faerie Queene* (Books I–III) published.
Sidney's *Arcadia* published.
Shakespeare's *HENRY VI*, Parts I–III,* *TITUS ANDRONICUS*.*
1591
Shakespeare's *RICHARD III*.*
1592
Marlowe's *DOCTOR FAUSTUS* and *EDWARD II*.*

Shakespeare's *TAMING OF THE SHREW** and *THE COMEDY OF ERRORS.**
Death of Greene.

1593

Shakespeare's *LOVE'S LABOR'S LOST;** *Venus and Adonis* published.
Death of Marlowe.
Theaters closed on account of plague.

1594

Shakespeare's *TWO GENTLEMEN OF VERONA;** *The Rape of Lucrece* published
Shakespeare's company becomes Lord Chamberlain's Men.
Death of Kyd.

1595

The Swan theater built.
Sidney's *Defense of Poesy* published.
Shakespeare's *ROMEO AND JULIET,** *A MIDSUMMER NIGHT'S DREAM,** *RICHARD II.**
Raleigh's first expedition to Guiana.

1596

Spenser's *Faerie Queene* (Books IV–VI) published.
Shakespeare's *MERCHANT OF VENICE,** *KING JOHN.**
James Shirley born.

1597

Bacon's *Essays* (first edition).
Shakespeare's *HENRY IV*, Part I.*

1598

Demolition of The Theatre.
Shakespeare's *MUCH ADO ABOUT NOTHING,** *HENRY IV*, Part II.*
Jonson's *EVERY MAN IN HIS HUMOR* (first version).
Seven books of Chapman's translation of Homer's *Iliad* published.

1599

The Paul's Boys reopen their theater.

The Globe theater opened.

Shakespeare's *AS YOU LIKE IT*,* *HENRY V*, *JULIUS CAESAR*.*

Marston's *ANTONIO AND MEL-LIDA*,* Parts I and II.

Dekker's *THE SHOEMAKERS' HOLIDAY*.*

Death of Spenser.

1600

Shakespeare's *TWELFTH NIGHT*.*

The Fortune theater built by Alleyn.

The Children of the Chapel begin to play at the Blackfriars.

1601

Shakespeare's *HAMLET*,* *MERRY WIVES OF WINDSOR*.*

Insurrection and execution of the Earl of Essex.

Jonson's *POETASTER*.

Brief residence at Oxford (?)

1602

Shakespeare's *TROILUS AND CRESSIDA*.*

Admitted to the Middle Temple, November 16.

1603

Death of Queen Elizabeth I; accession of James VI of Scotland as James I.

Florio's translation of Montaigne's *Essays* published.

Shakespeare's *ALL'S WELL THAT ENDS WELL*.*

Heywood's *A WOMAN KILLED WITH KINDNESS*.

Marston's *THE MALCONTENT*.*

Shakespeare's company becomes the King's Men.

1604

Shakespeare's *MEASURE FOR MEASURE*,* *OTHELLO*.*

Marston's *THE FAWN*.*

Chapman's *BUSSY D'AMBOIS.**

1605
Shakespeare's *KING LEAR.**
Marston's *THE DUTCH COUR-TESAN.**
Bacon's *Advancement of Learning* published.
The Gunpowder Plot.

Expelled from the Middle Temple for not paying buttery bill.

1606
Shakespeare's *MACBETH.**
Jonson's *VOLPONE.**
Tourneur's *REVENGER'S TRAG-EDY.**
The Red Bull theater built.
Death of John Lyly.

Publication of *Fame's Memorial* (poem) and *Honor Triumphant* (pamphlet).
Barnes's *Four Books of Offices*, with commendatory verses by Ford, and Cooper's *Funeral Tears for the Death of the Earl of Devonshire*, with a poem by Ford, published.

1607
Shakespeare's *ANTONY AND CLEOPATRA.**
Beaumont's *KNIGHT OF THE BURNING PESTLE.**
Settlement of Jamestown, Virginia.

1608
Shakespeare's *CORIOLANUS,* TIMON OF ATHENS,* PERIC-LES.**
Chapman's *CONSPIRACY AND TRAGEDY OF CHARLES, DUKE OF BYRON.**
Dekker's *Gull's Hornbook* published.
Richard Burbage leases Blackfriars Theatre for King's Company.
John Milton born.

Reinstated at the Middle Temple, June 10.

1609
Shakespeare's *CYMBELINE;** *Sonnets* published.
Jonson's *EPICOENE.*

1610
Jonson's *ALCHEMIST.*
Chapman's *REVENGE OF BUSSY D'AMBOIS.**
Richard Crashaw born.

Receives total bequest of £10 upon the death of his father, Thomas Ford.

1611

Authorized (King James) Version of the Bible published.
Shakespeare's *THE WINTER'S TALE*,* *THE TEMPEST*.*
Beaumont and Fletcher's *A KING AND NO KING*.
Tourneur's *ATHEIST'S TRAGEDY*.*
Middleton's *A CHASTE MAID IN CHEAPSIDE*.*
Chapman's translation of *Iliad* completed.

1612

Webster's *THE WHITE DEVIL*.*

1613

The Globe theater burned.
Shakespeare's *HENRY VIII* (with Fletcher).
Webster's *THE DUCHESS OF MALFI*,*
Sir Thomas Overbury murdered.

1614

The Globe theater rebuilt.
The Hope Theater built.
Jonson's *BARTHOLOMEW FAIR*.

1615

1616

Publication of Folio edition of Jonson's *Works*.
Chapman's *Whole Works of Homer*.
Death of Shakespeare.
Death of Beaumont.

1617

1618

Outbreak of Thirty Years War.
Execution of Raleigh.

Christ's Bloody Sweat (poem) and *The Golden Mean* (pamphlet) published.

Sir Thomas Overbury's Ghost (book; not extant) entered in the Stationers' Register, November 25.

Granted £20 per year by will of his older brother, Henry, September 17.

One of forty members of the Middle Temple admonished for wearing hats instead of lawyers' caps.

1620
Pilgrim Fathers land at Plymouth. *A Line of Life* (pamphlet) published.

1621
Middleton's *WOMEN BEWARE* *THE WITCH OF EDMONTON*,
*WOMEN.** with Dekker and Rowley.
Robert Burton's *Anatomy of Melan-
choly* published.
Andrew Marvell born.

1622
Middleton and Rowley's *THE
CHANGELING.**
Henry Vaughan born.

1623
Publication of Folio edition of *THE SPANISH GYPSY* (?), with
Shakespeare's *COMEDIES, HIST-* Middleton and Rowley (Lady
ORIES AND TRAGEDIES. Elizabeth's company).
Webster's *THE DUCHESS OF
MALFI* and Cockeram's *The English
Dictionary*, both with commendatory
verses by Ford, published.

1624 *THE SUN'S DARLING*, with Dekker, licensed by Herbert.
THE BRISTOW MERCHANT
(lost) and *THE FAIRY KNIGHT*
(lost [?]), both with Dekker.
*THE LATE MURDER OF THE
SON UPON THE MOTHER* (lost),
with Dekker, Rowley, and Webster.

1625
Death of King James I; accession of *THE FAIR MAID OF THE INN*,
Charles I. with Fletcher, Massinger, and
Death of Fletcher. Webster.

1626
Death of Tourneur.
Death of Bacon.

1627
Death of Middleton.

1628
Petition of Right. *THE LOVER'S MELANCHOLY*
Buckingham assassinated. (published 1629).

1629

Shirley's *THE WEDDING* and Massinger's *THE ROMAN ACTOR*, both with commendatory verses by Ford, published.

1630

BEAUTY IN A TRANCE * (lost).

1631
Shirley's *THE TRAITOR*.
Death of Donne.
John Dryden born.

1632
Massinger's *THE CITY MADAM*.*

Brome's *THE NORTHERN LASS*, with commendatory verses by Ford, published.

1633
Donne's *Poems* published.
Death of George Herbert.

THE BROKEN HEART, LOVE'S SACRIFICE, and *'TIS PITY SHE'S A WHORE* published.

1634
Death of Chapman, Marston, Webster.*
Publication of *THE TWO NOBLE KINSMEN*, with title-page attribution to Shakespeare and Fletcher.
Milton' *Comus*.

PERKIN WARBECK published.

1635
Sir Thomas Browne's *Religio Medici*.

1636

Massinger's *THE GREAT DUKE OF FLORENCE*, with commendatory verses by Ford, published.

1637
Death of Jonson.

1638

THE LADY'S TRIAL licensed.
THE FANCIES CHASTE AND NOBLE published.
Jonsonus Virbius, with commendatory verses by Ford, published.

1639
First Bishop's War.
Death of Carew.*

Publication of *THE LADY'S TRIAL*, with dedication signed by Ford.
No certain later record of Ford.

1640
Short Parliament.
Long Parliament impeaches Laud.
Death of Massinger, Burton.

1641
Irish rebel.
Death of Heywood.

1642
Charles I leaves London; Civil War breaks out.
Shirley's *COURT SECRET.*
All theaters closed by Act of Parliament.

1643
Parliament swears to the Solemn League and Covenant.

1645
Ordinance for New Model Army enacted.

1646
End of First Civil War.

1647
Army occupies London.
Charles I forms alliance with Scots.
Publication of Folio edition of Beaumont and Fletcher's
COMEDIES AND TRAGEDIES.

1648
Second Civil War.

1649
Execution of Charles I.

1650
Jeremy Collier born.

1651
Hobbes' *Leviathan* published.

1652
First Dutch War began (ended 1654).
Thomas Otway born.

1653
Nathaniel Lee born.*   *THE QUEEN* published.

1656
D'Avenant's *THE SIEGE OF RHODES* performed at Rutland House.

1657
John Dennis born.

1658
Death of Oliver Cromwell.
D'Avenant's *THE CRUELTY OF THE SPANIARDS IN PERU* performed at the Cockpit.

Howard's *THE GREAT FAVORITE, OR THE DUKE OF LERMA*, possibly a rewriting of some earlier play by Ford, published.

1660
Restoration of Charles II.
Theatrical patents granted to Thomas Killigrew and Sir William D'Avenant, authorizing them to form, respectively, the King's and the Duke of York's Companies.

AN ILL BEGINNING HAS A GOOD END (lost), *THE LONDON MERCHANT* (lost), and *THE ROYAL COMBAT* (lost) all entered in the Stationers' Register and attributed to Ford by Moseley.